This book is essen[illegible]ants and a must-read for any woma[illegible]h—too ambitious, too sensitive, or sir[illegible] empowers you to embrace your so-called "too-much-ness" and reimagine it in a unique new way. With step-by-step advice, Jessica emphasizes the importance of women building wealth, shedding perfectionism, and confidently charging their worth—"like a straight white guy!" And instead of running on fumes, you can "become like a fountain that is so full of water that it gushes over the sides..." and truly thrive unapologetically.

—Sherry Lukey, Executive and Life Coach

Becoming an entrepreneur is an immense journey of self-discovery. You suddenly don't have the support systems you relied on in your corporate life. And that journey is hard but enlightening. Jessica's approach holds your hand to help you realize what you are capable of. *Too Much* is a powerful tool for any female entrepreneur who has ever doubted herself.

—Patty Caballero, PSC Consulting

Reading this book felt like sitting in an extended session with Jessica, exploring what can keep me from stepping into my greatness. Her authentic voice leaps from every page and speaks to the deep-seated stories that we tell ourselves when we have come to believe that we're "too much." Jessica's words spoke to my soul, and the takeaways from the book are a powerful support to the work I've done with her as my coach, leading to incredible shifts in my business. I'll be recommending this book to so many other amazing women I know who are what this world needs in their "too-muchness!"

—Cynthia

Too Much is a gift to the reader. I found Jessica and her Seven Figures Club early in my consulting journey after 25 years in corporate. Little did I know how deeply and profoundly her approach would benefit my personal life and business. Dive into the coaching wisdom she drops in *Too Much*, and you will not emerge the same person, in the best, brightest, "exactly the right amount" way.

—Catherine Hamilton, Trestle Solutions

This book feels like a conversation with a friend who truly understands and celebrates you. Every page had me thinking, "Yes! That's exactly it!"—Jessica's words spoke directly to me, describing my childhood, adulthood, and life experiences in ways I've never been able to articulate. Her ability to capture feelings so many of us share but have struggled to express is nothing short of brilliant. Whether you're building a seven-figure business or simply striving to live authentically, this book serves as a guide to embracing your true self and finding deeper fulfillment in both life and work.

—Amanda HarNess Doyle

As a female independent consultant and a huge fan of Jessica's work, I knew I would probably love this book, but I did not anticipate the immediate shifts it created in my thinking. It is a must-read for women consultants, but probably also any other businesswomen or really anyone who has ever felt like "Too Much". The business books I usually read fall into one of these two categories: They contain an extensive project plan but do not address and handle any of the overwhelm, resistance, and countless other feelings that invariably come up for me while running and growing my business. Or they are personal stories, which are inspiring and provide identification, but putting them down, I always ask myself: "Now what?". Reading *Too Much* provides practical advice, lots of stories from Jessica's own journey and clients, and thereby gave me the tools to put my inner critic in its place and truly dream and go big!

—Christina Brauer, Capital C

Too Much by Jessica Fearnley hits home. If you have spent any time believing that you have to play smaller than you feel inside—it is the perfect read. Jessica guides you through a journey of self-discovery, helping you break free from the limiting narratives you hold and showing you how entrepreneurship can be a space where your true, unapologetic self can shine. With openness and authenticity, she shares her personal story, providing key insights on achieving fulfillment, releasing what holds you back, and realizing that designing the life you desire is more achievable than you think. If you've ever questioned whether you're "too much" and felt the weight of holding yourself back, this book is for you. It's a powerful book you'll keep coming back to, with pages marked, dog-eared, and filled with personal insights.

—Victoria Hatfield, The Growth Plan LLC

This book speaks to every overachieving woman entrepreneur I know—including me! It addresses the mindset junk we carry in ways that we absolutely have to tackle as women business owners, but in a safe and accepting manner. I recommend this book for any woman entrepreneur who knows it's about so much more than spreadsheets, accepting the mediocre and doing "just enough to get by." From "too much" to always the right amount, Jessica gives us permission to be who we are and heal from a past that no longer serves us. Onward to seven figures and beyond, ladies!

—Tara McDonagh, Tara McDonagh Communications

As someone who has really benefitted from Jessica's wisdom and insights as a coach, I'm delighted that others now get to benefit from her experience too. Her book offers great advice for all of us who've been told we're too much and gives us a permission slip to be exactly who we are and were meant to be.

—Niven

This book is packed with powerful insights. Jessica tackles the paradox of feeling "too much" and "not enough," overtly calling out the societal pressures to not overshadow colleagues or male bosses, and the surprising link between hiding your gifts and burnout. Her chapter on trauma is essential for high achievers, exploring its impact with clarity and relief—there is a lot of power in how she unpacks it. ALL of it helps you find the places where you've been working harder to fit in, make what you want to make, and build what you want to build and then shows you how to find a more true, more fun, more productive path where you get better results by working less because you're leveraging all your gifts and not hiding from what you really want. Having worked with Jessica as my business coach, I was blown away by how impactful this book is—she combines deep empathy with practical, actionable guidance in every chapter.

—Alecia Huck, MAVERICK & Company

TOO MUCH

JESSICA FEARNLEY

Peacock Feather Publishing
Sheffield, United Kingdom

Too Much

DISCLAIMER: The information in this book is intended for educational and entertainment purposes only. This book is not intended to be a substitute for the legal, medical, psychological, accounting, or finance advice of a professional. Any use of the information in this book is at the reader's discretion and risk. The author and publisher are not offering professional services advice. Additionally, this book is not intended to serve as the basis for any financial or business decisions. You should seek the services of a competent professional, especially if you need expert assistance for your specific situation.

Success stories and results shared do not guarantee future results or performance. While best efforts have been made in preparing this book, the author and publisher make no warranty, representation, or guarantee with respect to the accuracy or completeness of the information contained herein.

The author and publisher assume no responsibility for your actions and specifically disclaim responsibility for any liability, loss, risk or any physical, psychological, emotional, financial, or commercial damages, personal or otherwise, which is incurred as a consequence, directly or indirectly, of the use and application of any of the contents of this book.

Seven Figure Consultant Limited
jessicafearnley.com

ISBN 978-1-0683767-0-2 (paperback)
ISBN 978-1-0683767-1-9 (ebook)
ISBN 978-1-0683767-2-6 (audiobook)

Cover Design: Bloom and Brave Creative
Book Design: Clarity Designworks

Special discounts are available on quantity purchases by corporations, associations and others. For details, contact the publisher.

To my clients and my Seven Figures Club Ladies, past, present and future. I am humbled and honored to be your coach and your guide on the journey.

I love seeing for each of you the spark of inspiration becoming more and more fulfilled with every month that goes by, and the money showing up as a result! This book is for you—and all the women across the world who need to hear this message.

To all the coaches, counsellors and therapists who have been part of my journey these last 25 years. Thank you for helping me piece this together one fragment at a time. I am forever grateful.

jessicafearnley.com

jessicafearnley.com/linkedin

@sevenfigureconsultant

Download your book bonuses here: jessicafearnley.com/bonus

Contents

PART THREE

PART ONE

What 'Too Much' Really Means

(It might not be what you think...)

Introduction: It's Not You

I am someone who has often felt like I am too much.

In my education. In my career. In my relationships.

From who I am as a person, to what I seek to achieve in life, to how I go about achieving it.

My ambition. My curiosity. My drive to go deeper. My unwillingness to hold back or slow down, because what I really want to do in every situation is jump in with both feet and give it 1000%. Even when my own body can't keep up.

I am too much. I think I may have been too much from the moment I was born. My mother says I was a very spirited baby and toddler, who got notably less frustrated once I could talk and write. Adolescent me got good grades, wanted to write novels and be in a rock band. Adult me showed tremendous promise at university and was tipped for big things in my corporate career. But I always felt like too much at school, at university and in the workplace. I felt like too much in my family and with quite a few of my friends and the people I met. And then an episode of severe burnout in my late 20s meant my career plans got put on indefinite pause. All the momentum I had built up came to a grinding halt, and it felt like my road had run out. It took time to see it, but I had to learn a new way of doing life and work where my too-much-ness wasn't a liability but an asset. I had to learn a new way to hold it so that I wasn't frustrated, unappreciated, and always being asked to make myself smaller.

If you've picked up this book, I'm willing to bet that the label of 'too much' is something that resonates for you too. Maybe it's a label that someone attached to you when you were young. Maybe it has felt like it's stayed with you into your adult life and whatever you do, it always seems to come back to having other people find you to be too much.

Too much can be a compliment. *"Oh, you're too much!"* Said with laughter and glee. But I'm talking about the other kind of too much—the kind that sort of makes it feel like there is something wrong with you. You are different to other people. Too lively. Too opinionated. Too ambitious. Too emotional. Too sensitive. You are too much for other people. You tire them out or perplex them with your multi-faceted way of looking at the world, or your complex emotions. It has probably shown up in your career, your education, your family, your friendships, your romantic relationships. And it hurts. *Why do I feel so fragile when others seem so robust? Why do I get it wrong so often? Why do I face so much rejection and feel like a misfit in the rooms that others seem to be comfortable in? Why do I always have to rein myself in and not come across as too much, when others seem to be able to be their authentic selves without causing any drama? What is so dangerous about being my whole self? Why does it feel so exposing and vulnerable to put my true self on full view?*

What if Too Much Doesn't Mean what You Think it Does?

This book is going to show you that in the best possible way, you have got it wrong when it comes to being too much, because too much doesn't mean what you think it does. They say you can't read the label from inside the jar, and from where you've been sitting for possibly a lot of your life to this point, 'too much' feels like a pretty lousy jar to have been given. But I'm going to show you that it's the best thing in the world to be too much, because it's the signpost to the life and business you are supposed to have. Sure, there are some tricky parts to life when you're too much. It hurts to be the black sheep, the person who naturally breaks toxic cycles and patterns in your family, your workplace, wherever else you might find them. It's actually a brilliant thing to be the person who puts an end to these things instead of passing them down to the next generation, but I get why it probably hasn't felt that way until now.

About Me

In case we haven't met already, I'm Jessica, and I'm a business coach who helps consultant women grow their business from 6 to 7 figures. And guess what. A seven figure revenue is considered by many women entrepreneurs to be a *goal* that is too much. So it makes perfect sense that for ambitious women who are too much, seven figures is actually a goal that is just the right amount. And that is what this book is here to help you discover—when you find the right context for your too-much-ness, you realize that far from being too much, you are exactly the right amount.

But to give you a bit of context in terms of who I am and how I've come to write this book, I'm a Brit, but I do the bulk of my coaching work with women in the USA. I also work with women in the UK, Canada, Middle East, South Africa, Australia and Europe. I'm a Highly Sensitive Person, an Enneagram 4, a Wealth Dynamics *Creator* profile, and a Myers-Briggs INFJ. But funnily enough, I didn't understand a lot of these things about myself until relatively recently. I'm now in my early 40s, have been happily married for 15 years and have two elementary school aged sons, plus two cats and a dog. These days I feel confident and fulfilled in my work. I'm comfortable in my own skin, and I know how to play to my strengths. I understand why certain situations don't work for me, and I'm ok with that. I see my gifts and abilities and don't feel the need to minimize them, or to make myself smaller for other people.

But in my teens, 20s and 30s, it was a different story. One where I felt the stigma of being too much without also seeing the gift that it is to be too much. And my burnout episode at 27 was the turning point where I realized I had been living out my too-much-ness in all the wrong ways. I did well at school, but I think most of us find the 'teenage girl' phase hard to navigate and I was always very aware that I didn't like the same things a lot of girls did, and I liked the things I liked way more than I was meant to. While school friends were going crazy for manufactured boy bands, I was obsessed with indie music—I would spend hours poring over song lyrics and listening to albums on repeat to pick up every nuance of the songs I liked. I wasn't that into mainstream culture or fashion, and although I tried, I never felt like I really fit.

I didn't go to college right away after finishing school, because I was in a rock band I had started with my best friends from school and wanted to see where it would go. I worked a day job for 3 years around gigging with my band evenings and weekends, before finally enrolling to study History at a good university 150 miles away when I was 21. I had been scared to leave my life at home and take the leap, but realized straightaway that I loved the freedom to pursue my academic interests. It was an environment where I excelled because I could run as far and as fast as I wanted. I loved building out a bibliography and going the extra mile to source obscure references for footnotes. I got better grades than a lot of my coursemates but quickly found it was better not to say much about my exam and essay successes. People were pleased for me initially, but beyond a certain point it all felt a bit awkward. I knew I had a shot at getting a First class degree classification, and I worked incredibly hard and did go on to get it. But it created a gap between us, and I couldn't help feeling that it would have been easier socially if I wasn't wired to be so ambitious or had managed to tone it down a little. I felt lonely at times, but I didn't want to have to choose between honoring my too-much-ness or under-achieving so I felt more *like* other people.

I took a job in project management in London after graduating, and quickly found that it was a brilliant environment to progress and hone my skills. I was eager to get ahead, but corporate culture was a shock to my system. We worked in a huge open plan office, and most of our conversations happened through meetings that had to be arranged over email in advance. I was suddenly a tiny cog in a huge wheel, and I really struggled with the lack of freedom compared to my academic studies, *and* the slow pace that everything seemed to move at. I was often under-utilized, but was required to be present in the office all day every day, looking busy even though I often wasn't and longed to be. My colleagues had no idea, but in terms of my mental and physical health, I was hanging on by a thread.

I was good at my job and was sought after for key projects at work, with fantastic mentors who were helping me climb the ladder. But I felt like I was way too much for the level of work I was allowed to do. When I didn't have much work going on, I would often put myself forward for projects only to be knocked back because *"you haven't been here long enough"* or *"we only want people above your grade"*. It was doubly frustrating for me because I was 3 years older than others in my cohort, and I had worked as a project manager before I went to college so I had more experience than people often realized. But ultimately, I was bored and restless. I was becoming sick. And it became harder and harder to keep showing up as if none of it was affecting me. My body was shutting down, showing signs of exhaustion and burnout, but that wasn't a word that had been invented at that point and I didn't have a clue how to help myself.

I hit burnout in February 2010. I still remember the morning that my alarm went off, and instead of dragging myself up and into the office, I felt something snap inside of me. I switched off my alarm.

"*No.*" My body said. "*I can't do it anymore.*" And I found myself in floods of tears, as the exhaustion finally took over and I realized I had reached the end of my ability to keep pushing forward. I received sick pay for several months, but I couldn't overcome my burnout and would get exhausted and totally overwhelmed at even the thought of returning to the same job. I also couldn't face the thought of looking for another corporate role elsewhere.

Later that year my employer announced voluntary lay-offs after the organization lost a chunk of critical funding, and I applied and was accepted. I became unemployed. And I had no clue what I was going to do with my life. It was my ground zero. But it was also the beginning of doing life differently and rebuilding it one fragment at a time. Not for the benefit of other people but for the first time, with my authentic self in full view.

I now knew what it was to make myself sick from trying to be too small and just trying to white-knuckle through my frustration at being under-fulfilled in my career. But in the process, I had lost my spark and at that point, I didn't think I would ever regain it. My too much had become 'nothing special', and I honestly believed I was on the scrap heap for life. But that wasn't the end of my story.

After a seven month break from work, I started a fairly junior role working for an occupational psychology consultancy start-up based in Islington, London. It became clear that with my background in project management and business planning and development, I had more to offer than just basic admin, and I ended up becoming Number 2 in the business and playing a key role in growing the fledgling company from six to seven figures across four years. In that fourth year, the company was sold. Meanwhile I had just had my first baby and I was ready for a new challenge. I craved going back to a smaller business context, but I didn't know if I could easily find a role that would suit my unicorn skillset or offer the flexibility I had gotten used to. "*I'm good at growing businesses*", I remember thinking, *"but that's not a thing—who on earth would hire me to do that?!"* Somehow, I stumbled across the idea of becoming a business coach but at first I may as well have been trying to become a Martian. I knew business but I wasn't a coach, and in fact I first called myself a 'business consultant'. But everyone I met through networking would just say, *"Oh, Jessica? She's a business coach!"* More that that, I started to noticed that my clients often knew what to do, but they still found themselves not taking any action, and actually I could serve them better by coaching them through their resistance alongside advising them on business strategy. So eventually I stopped fighting it, leaned into coaching, realized I was obsessed with it and actually kind of good at it, and 10 years later—here I am.

Along the journey of the last decade, I have battled countless mindset monkeys, a vast array of limiting beliefs, all kinds of business catastrophes and crises, but mostly because I was too stubborn to give up, have ended up with a coaching business I love, serving clients I am in awe of, and most importantly, helping them come to a deeper sense of fulfillment in life and business while making more money than they have ever dreamed of. Although I feared that I had lost the spark that made me too much, I have been able to find it again. And when I look back over the last few years, I can see that my feeling of being too much has actually become the feeling of being just the right amount. Too much doesn't have to be a stigma when we know how to hold it. It's actually a great thing to be too much, and more than that, I wouldn't be able to do the work I now do if I wasn't. So, what follows in this book are some of the things I have learned on the journey from 'too much' to 'just the right amount'. And I would love to share these insights with you as a fellow 'too-much-er'.

What You'll Get from Reading this Book

Honestly, I'm way too impatient and when I'm reading a book I usually skip over the content summary but I know that some of you like to know where our journey is heading (and rightly so)—so here goes:

I know my high-achievers always want to get to the answers straightaway, but Part One is going to be a bit of a mind expansion as we explore holding our too-much-ness differently. We are going to explore what it truly means to be too much and the reasons why this is actually a good thing. We're also going to zoom in and look at the impact of having trauma in your backstory, and then zoom out and look at the need in the wider world for more women to be living in pursuit of self-actualization and creating wealth.

In Part Two, we're getting practical and tactical. We're going to explore how to look for your 'more'. I will set out my 3 step blueprint for pursuing peak fulfillment—*Connecting, Dealing and Feeling*—and walk you through how to put this into practice in your life and business.

And then in Part Three, we're going to be troubleshooting once you are on the road to discovering your 'more'. We're going to look at letting go of 'hard' and allowing business and life to be easy. I'm excited for every word I've written in this book, but Part Three is where we really get to the good stuff because I'm going to be giving you a sneak preview of some of the real-life bumps in the road that start to happen when you set out on your journey from too much to just the right amount. Forewarned is forearmed, so we're going to make doubly sure you have everything you need to not get knocked off-course.

I would love you to feel that reading this book is like an awesome virtual coffee together. They say that you are the sum of the five people you spend the most time with, and let's just say I would love for you to feel like you can add me to your crew for the duration of reading this book. I'm giving it all the abundance energy I have and I hope this lights a fire for you as you read it.

And I want to say right off the bat—this book is for women who are serious about becoming seven figure entrepreneurs. The world needs more of us. Does this mean that everyone needs to be a seven figure entrepreneur? No, it definitely doesn't. If you are reading this book and up to now, nodding along with every word but don't have a business or don't want to grow your business, you are absolutely welcome to be here. But part of my mission in the world is to hold space for ambitious women entrepreneurs who want to take over the world and still be back in time for dinner. This is actually why I love to work with women B2B consultants who serve corporates. It happens to be the kind of business that I have the most practical hands-on experience with—but if you are an ex-senior corporate leader, you might not already know that consulting is one of the easiest arenas where you can create a seven figure business based around your corporate expertise. Seven figures can be so straightforward for consultants, and yet so many women who more than meet the requirements don't realize this.

There is much more to say about this, but suffice to say for now, I am going to be unapologetic with you throughout this book for holding space for seven figure women consultants. There are plenty of books out there for women who haven't started a business yet. But this book is for six and seven figure women consultants who know that seven figures is the minimum they are willing to receive. We need more honest conversations about seven figure businesses and what really happens when you move past the low six figures. As women entrepreneurs, it can often feel like way too much for us to have seven figure ambitions and I'm all about putting an end to that. We need to normalize the aspiration of a seven figure business. After all, something you may not know is the definition of a small business in the USA is revenue of less than—wait for it—$50M with fewer than 50 employees. Do you see how much room that gives us to be aspiring to $1M and more? A $1M revenue is still barely scratching the surface of what it means to be a small business, so there is no reason why we should feel like it's too much to aspire to or expect from ourselves.

But this isn't just a conversation about money—we ultimately feel the sting of 'too-much-ness' at an emotional, behavioral and existential level. We put ourselves in the wrong rooms and then feel stigmatized and misunderstood. So, we're going to going to go back to basics and explore what it truly means to be too much so that you can stop feeling shame at being too much, and instead wear it as the badge of honor it absolutely is.

Imagine how your life and business would be if instead of feeling like too much, you felt like the right amount. That instead of feeling pressure to go slower or make yourself smaller, you could do life as fast as you wanted, or as loudly as you wanted, with the color saturation turned up as high as you dream of and no limits to your creativity or confidence. Imagine if you found the places where it suddenly made so much sense that you are the way you are, and instead of feeling that pressure to be less, you were celebrated and recognized by your industry and peers for being the fullest extent of yourself. That is the goal of this book. If you feel like too much, it is time to own it. *"Yes I am too much. And I'm proud of myself for that!"*. That is what I want for everyone reading this book. It's not about you needing to experience MY journey, but using what I have learned to fuel YOUR journey. I would love for you to go far beyond where I have been because I'm not the hero of this story—you are. And I'm here to be your guide and mentor, if you'll have me.

So. Are you ready for the ride of your life?

Let's jump in.

1 Reimagining Too Much

(Because, by the way, You're Awesome!)

If Too Much is a Gift, What's the Returns Policy?

You could be forgiven for feeling this based on your experience of being too much so far! How on earth could being too much actually be a good thing. Let alone a gift? Here's an important couple of questions we need to ask to help us get our heads around it:

Ok so if I'm too much, WHAT am I too much for?
Or WHO am I too much for?

And this will be our focus in this chapter. We are going to look at where the notion of too much comes from, how it manifests for us and intersects with our biggest fears about ourselves. We're also going to look at what happens when we try and squash down our too-much-ness and play small, and I'm going to reveal the biggest reframe we need in order to start holding our too-much-ness differently.

So let's dive in with where the notion of too much comes from. And I'm going to put on my historian's hat for a moment, because there is a huge historical precedent that we need to acknowledge so we can understand the enormity of what we are dealing with here. And here it is:

Women Aren't Supposed to Take Up Space

For thousands of years, women have been expected to do life from within very narrow parameters. *Madonna* or *Whore. Wife and Mother* or *Old Maid.* It hasn't been possible for women to live multi-faceted lives, and we will dig more into this in Chapter 5. We are starting to see some progress (although not nearly enough). But we still bear the legacy of the past in the conditioning and programming today's women and girls receive, in the form of strict rules for where women are allowed to be and how we are allowed to conduct ourselves. Women have been required to be quiet and deferential to males and patriarchs and the societal structures that uphold them. Alongside this, it has been considered improper for women to buck these trends, and the ones that did paid a huge price for it—societal shame, physical violation, and even paying for it with their lives.[1] Historically in much of Europe and North America, women were not able to own land, or their own material possessions until well into the nineteenth century,[2] let alone vote[3], or get degrees[4], or work as a doctor[5] or in the military[6]. Women did not have equal access to credit until the late twentieth century.[7] Even in the twenty-first century, women are still the poor relation when it comes to crucial elements of financial equity such as pensions and equal pay.[8] You may have heard the statistic that there are more male CEOs named John than women CEOs in the USA, which only ceased to be the case in 2023.[9] And as I'm sure you are all too aware, most recently in the USA, reproductive rights and body autonomy for women has been repealed in several states and may even be further restricted in the years ahead.

With all of this in mind, if you are a woman and you are being given the label of too much, well, frankly—it shows you are doing something right. You are going against the grain of history. Because when the world requires women to be small and insignificant, we as women who are too much are living proof that women are not 'less than' men. The gifts and abilities of women who are too much show how shallow and reductive the stereotypes around the inferiority of women truly are. And we can either shrink ourselves down to comply and perpetuate the things that women have been historically denied or excluded from, or we can choose to take up space and challenge the status quo. The world needs women who are too much. And it needs us to ask, "*wait, why does this still happen?*" And to point out inequity, and question, "*why do we do things this way?*" OF COURSE women who are too much are a threat to the patriarchy. And we need to stand in that with our heads held high. As I stated in the introduction, we need to own this. *"Yes, I am too much. And I'm proud of it!"*

So now that we've seen the historical roots of too-much-ness, why does it often apply to women like us?

You Are Too Much Because You Are Gifted

In order to understand how too-much-ness manifests for us, we need to grapple with this truth, which tell us what lies at the heart of being too much AND explains why it is such a sticking point. In the simplest of terms, being too much is a gift because it means you are GIFT-ed. Even if it feels hard to admit that to yourself. It's not because you're too intense, or because it's unreasonable of you to want more. We need to stop putting the wrong label on the situation. You are not too much because you are weird or different or 'other'. There's a reason you don't fit inside the narrow box you are supposed to—and it's because you are '*more than*' other people's expectations. Intellectually. Creatively. In whatever way it might manifest for you.

It comes down to giftedness. And you probably don't need me to point this out, but let's be real—being a gifted woman attracts the label of 'too much' like nothing else. When we are gifted, it can go one of two ways. You either feel proud of your gifts, because you realize or it is made obvious to you that this means you are special and it is a good thing, even if it can add some pressure at times to 'live up to your potential'. Your gifts are nurtured and you benefit from the many opportunities that open up for you because of your abilities. Or—you feel uncomfortable and embarrassed, and receive your giftedness as a stigma. Something that makes it impossible to blend in, something can be a huge frustration and source of internal conflict, and even something that makes you a target for bullying or unkind attention.

Can you remember the first time you realized that it wasn't a good thing to sparkle? When you were criticized, or dismissed, or told you were making other people look bad, or made fun of, for seeing the world in a million different colors instead of only black or white? Or creating too many layers of complexity in anything and everything? Or told you were 'overthinking'? Maybe, like me, you have been told you are 'too much' for as long as you can remember. As a child, I had so many ideas, opinions, questions, demands and creative solutions to everything. I was so persistent that my family gave me the nickname *"Jessica Pest-ica."* I was academically gifted and a natural musician. I learned to read and write quickly, and I would churn out pages of work at school, especially creative writing. I was curious about everything, and I was painfully honest in my judgements and opinions.

By the time I was in a corporate career, I was still too much. In more than one job, I got in trouble for working too fast. For being too productive. Because *"you are doing more than everyone and people don't like it."* I have always been bright, a quick study, able to see the problems straightaway, eager to please my superiors (in other words, a huge teacher's pet but I'm just going to own it—LOL), and when I feel that spark of curiosity for something, my energy is boundless. I'm guessing that you are wired the same way. I've never really understood why someone wouldn't give a task 110%. Or why it would be a good thing to dumb down my natural abilities, even though I've seen many women do this in the workplace over the years. But I'll be the first to admit that my 'giftedness' isn't particularly fair. I was born this way. It's a gift we receive, not one we necessarily earn.

But whether you feel like you deserve it or not, I'm going to state it again—being too much is a gift because it means you are gift-ed. There is something special about you that means you naturally stand out from the crowd. And because we live in a world where women receive a huge amount of pushback for acknowledging our brilliance—from men, from other women, but also parents, siblings, peers at school, colleagues at work, and even ourselves—this ends up meaning that, instead of being celebrated for our giftedness, all too often we feel shame because of it. And whether we are a kid in grade school or an adult in the workplace, we receive the message—*"I need to make myself smaller and not take up too much space"*. But there is another characteristic that intersects with our too-much-ness, and this is the notion of whether we are recognized as special.

Too Much and Special-ness

For those of us who are too much, our 'special-ness' matters. It may be that you're reading this and you don't immediate identify with the label of 'gifted'. Does it push buttons for you to suggest even just to yourself that you are 'more than' your surroundings? I meet women all the time who are doing the most amazing things in their businesses, and yet still, somehow, see themselves as 'nothing special'. Sometimes, we are lucky enough to have the right people in our lives at the right time, whether parents, teachers, friends, or bosses, who see our light and make us aware of it, but if you're someone who has had all the wrong labels put on you throughout your life, it is totally understandable that maybe you haven't realized even now how much your too-much-ness is a byproduct of how gifted and special you are. For me, the penny didn't really drop until I was 19 and in my first job out of school. I should have applied to college at that point—I got good grades in high school—but so did lots of kids at my school. I didn't think I was anything special. And consequently this meant I was living the wrong life.

Because I believed I was nothing special, I took a 9-5 job that didn't require me to be special—as a hospital administrator handling complaints in a failing health trust. My plan was to be an administrator by day and a rock guitar legend by night. I was in a band and we spent our evenings and weekends playing shows around the country. Rock music was my Plan A and my hospital job paid the bills. One day, my boss's boss called me to her office and asked me to sit down. My heart was pounding in my chest. Despite my toned-down-for-work goth makeup and rebel attitude I was still enough of a people pleaser that I didn't want to get reprimanded or fired. As I walked to her office, I was replaying the last few weeks at work and trying to think if I'd done anything that might be about to get me in trouble. But she didn't want to haul me over the coals, she had a proposal for me. *"I've noticed your work,"* she said. *"It's really good. And I'm going to help you. We're doing a restructure and I want to give you a new role."* She handed me a printed letter. *"This is the role, and this is your salary."* I blinked in shock as I read it. I was being promoted several grades up, to a top-level administrator. And the salary was a number I had never even dreamed of. I was ecstatic. But I was also baffled. What on earth had she seen in me? That was the first time someone had seen my potential but it wasn't the last, and I'm willing to bet that you've had this experience too, even if you haven't fully joined the dots yet on what this means about how exceptional you truly are.

Too Much.... or Not Enough?

A paradox I have noticed in women who feel like they are too much is that alongside our angst at being too much, we also have a huge fear that we are not enough. Maybe as you read this, you are still not totally sure you can say you are gifted or special. Isn't that just arrogance, or delusion? And this is perfectly rational, because so many of us have grown up in family cultures where our giftedness wasn't overtly acknowledged or encouraged. Whether it's fear of making other siblings look bad or feel inferior, or not wanting us to get too big for our boots or big-headed, to just not really knowing what to make of it all. Most of us were raised before self esteem was established as an important facet of parenting! We might have an inkling that we have always been intelligent and quick, but have we met the acceptance criteria for truly being 'gifted'? If you grew up feeling like this, you will likely have internalized this uncertainty which leads to deep discomfort—*what if I'm wrong and I'm not particularly gifted or special, I'm just an average Joe who works really hard?* And honestly, this fear DRIVES our high achievement. Because there is no set criteria for what it means to be gifted—and the people in our lives have rarely said it to us with conviction—our whole lives become one long quest to prove something we are not sure truly belongs to us.

So let's have a little checklist moment. *Are you smart? Did you get top grades at school?* Maybe you are thinking of all the people at your school who got better grades. *Were you amazing in your corporate career?* Maybe you're thinking of all the colleagues you felt were doing a better job than you were. *Are you awesome in your consulting work?* Maybe you're thinking of all the other entrepreneurs who make more money than you and worse, make it look easy. This is what is known as 'all or nothing thinking' and this isn't the only time we will meet this on our journey. It tends to go: *If I'm not the best, I'm probably the worst. Or just average.* I've dined out on this a lot and as an Enneagram 4 it has really pained me to NOT feel special in certain seasons of life. At times I have deeply feared that I am mistaken to believe I am gifted. As a competitive person, I feel crushed to not be the best or to see the evidence that others are better at something than I am. But I've had to learn to hold this better, because it's NOT all or nothing. You're not the worst if you're not in the number one spot. There are so many degrees in between! It's not the case that the only options are being the best or nothing special. When I was an undergrad on a course of 300 students I was in the top 10 or 15 results at graduation. For years I felt like this made me nothing special because I wasn't in the top 3. And honestly, how dumb is that?! Because at the very least, life is not built around school and university grades, and the quality and richness of life is not held only for the top achievers. I got a first-class undergraduate degree and a distinction in my Masters and honestly? No one has ever asked! But if we minimize our achievements through all or nothing thinking, and feel uncertain of our giftedness or our special-ness, it follows that too-much-ness will also feel deeply uncomfortable to us.

Playing Small and Burnout

So because it doesn't always feel good to be gifted, and several layers underneath all of this, we aren't always sure we *are* actually gifted, women who are too much can end up working hard to hide our gifts. You know that feeling that you are annoying someone with your bright sparkiness or your thoughts are flowing too fast, or you feel the eye roll in the room when you're yet again the first person to speak or be called upon in a meeting. Like, if you could just stand out less, it would make everyone else feel better about themselves and act better towards you. You would belong more if you were less exceptional. And when we believe that WE are the problem, it opens up a whole new set of problems.

I have met a lot of women in business and in life who play down their strengths and abilities to not stand out. Some take it a bridge further and play dumb, pretending to not understand something they clearly do understand, or adopting a self-deprecating stance. *"Me? I never understand anything! I'm such a hot mess!"* Others just blend into the background and take care not to draw the wrong kind of attention to themselves, because not everyone likes powerful, self-actualized women. And we have to be honest that our society does still frown upon women who shine bright. As the Japanese proverb goes, '*The nail that sticks out will be hammered in*,' and we all know the reality that there are consequences for failing to dim your light.

There is a danger for all girls and women that the structural messages we receive throughout our education and our corporate careers are that, before all else, we need to not pose a threat to others with our brilliance—especially to men, and even more so if they are older and whiter than us. It is better to be liked and accepted than to fulfill our ultimate potential. And I have seen this playing out for so many women in the workplace, but also as mothers, as entrepreneurs. But the problem is that when we hide our light and make ourselves smaller, we are living out of integrity with ourselves. It causes serious problems to our physical and mental health when we conceal things about ourselves and don't allow our gifts to come to fruition. This is estimated to be a leading cause of burnout—a phenomenon which is now endemic in Western society.[10]

I was shocked to discover that there is literally a thing in the educational world called a "Gifted and Talented Underachiever" where students who do not have the opportunity to live out their potential develop low self esteem and high levels of self-criticism and, instead of feeling proud of their accomplishments, they spiral downwards and can end up chronically depressed, even suicidal.[11] When our gifts are not recognized or nurtured, when we are not 'seen', it impacts our mental health and physical wellbeing. Women are lost from the corporate workplace in increasing numbers as they get older[12], and the reasons are multi-factorial. Lack of childcare, workplace bullying, sexual harassment, poor understanding of menopause and peri-menopause absolutely play a role. But I want to make the case that in the most simple terms, this happens to gifted women who go on to become consultants because we have been required to make ourselves too small for too long.

Not WHO but WHERE

The thing that we get wrong, when we feel shame at being too much, is that we think the problem is WHO we are, when, in reality, the problem is WHERE we are. It's not that you are too much period. It's that you are too much for your current situation, because the people there need you to be less, for reasons that likely belong to them and are not about you. And that isn't good for you. You shouldn't have to change yourself, or play smaller, and moreover, you don't need to.

I would love to introduce you to a mantra that will really help to hold our too-much-ness in the right way as we go through our journey together:

> ***When I feel like too much. It means THIS is not enough. Which means I need to look for more.***

You may have lived all of your life to this point believing that the equation goes like this:

When I feel like too much → it means I am too much → which means I am a horrible person → which means SHAME SHAME SHAME. Why can't I be like everyone else? Why am I so needy? *crisis*

So, let's examine this together for a moment.

When I feel like too much. It means THIS is not enough. Which means I need to look for more.

The thing you need to change is WHERE you are showing up. In your corporate career this might have meant working in a different team or for a better boss. It might mean you needed a mentor who wasn't threatened by your giftedness. It might mean you needed to pursue a different career. It might mean that, like me and the women I work with, your dream life lies in being your own boss. It might mean that you aim to be in the top 2% of women entrepreneurs who build seven figure businesses, which shouldn't be a controversial goal, but often is—even in exclusively female online safe spaces for business.

I'm going to state this here in case no one in your life ever has:

YOU are not the problem. It's not who you are, it's where you are.

Because when you are in the right place, your too-much-ness suddenly feels like just the right amount. And so if you feel like too much at the moment, or if you've felt like too much for most of your life, I want to suggest that it's because you've been in the wrong places with the wrong people. When you can surround yourself with people who celebrate your contributions instead of feeling threatened by them, you don't need to keep looking over your shoulder to make sure that you're not annoying people or talking too much. When you can align your gifts with people and places where your abilities are lauded as an asset rather than hidden as a liability, you don't have to pretend to be less to fit in. And for the women I work with, consulting is an excellent avenue to pursue because it offers a brilliant context for you to showcase your giftedness. It's where you can prove your too-much-ness makes you an asset, not a liability. Consulting is a context where you discover—finally!—it pays to be quick and opinionated and insightful.

We've covered a lot of ground in this chapter! But now that you've understood where your feelings of too much come from, how they manifest and how they intersect with our biggest fears about ourselves, we're going to explore a big concept you have probably heard of many times, but have never connected to your struggle with being too much.

See you there!

CHAPTER 1 SUMMARY

- » If Too Much is a Gift, What's the Returns Policy?
- » Women Aren't Supposed to Take Up Space
- » You Are Too Much Because You Are Gifted
- » Too Much and Special-ness
- » Too Much.... or Not Enough?
- » Playing Small and Burnout
- » Not WHO but WHERE

2 It All Comes Down to Fulfillment

At the end of the last chapter I made a pretty big claim—that I'm going to show you a big concept that you will definitely have heard of many times, but that you probably haven't ever connected to your struggle with feeling like too much. And here it is:

Fulfillment.

The concept of fulfillment is a really important part of the whole discussion around feeling like too much. Fulfillment is the lens we need to be looking through so that, instead of simply deciding we are the problem because we are too much, we can start to identify where we are being called to instead.

In this chapter we are going to explore fulfillment and its impact on your too-much-ness. We're also going to see what it looks like when we fall into a distorted version of too much that isn't good for us or the people around us. We'll learn the antidote to that so we can focus on thriving as too much—and feeling like just the right amount—instead of spending life just trying to survive.

It All Comes Down to Fulfillment

What is fulfillment? It is the feeling that you are doing the thing or things that everything in your life has been building up to. It is the universal *"This is why. THIS is what I was made for."* Fulfillment means learning how to hold our intellectual gifts so that they don't destroy us, but instead light the path we were always intended to follow in life. And it is nearly always accompanied by recognition from others—the standing ovation, the tears of resonance, the feeling that something we have seen or heard feels deeply meaningful and meant for us. We know we have found fulfillment when our words or actions profoundly move others, and in turn, this profoundly moves us.

When we understand fulfillment correctly and learn to follow the trail of breadcrumbs our intuition is sending us every moment of every day, everything starts to change. Lots of us, as ambitious women, create an arbitrary life plan at a relatively young age, when we have very little self-awareness and have discovered very little about who we actually are. I know I did this. We decide we will do X career and follow this path until we are very successful [insert happy ending here]. The End. And then after five, ten, or twenty years of following this path, you realize that you aren't actually feeling fulfilled. You don't love your life. You don't like your career. Everything feels very disconnected. And it can feel like a problem with no solution. But fulfillment isn't just an all or nothing concept (see, I told you we would run into this again!)—it's a helpful barometer of how we are doing on different days and in different seasons of our lives. But how can you identify how fulfilled you are on any given day? Isn't this like trying to tell if you have a stomach ache by watching a weather report?

I discovered an answer to this from an unexpected source, in the work by Don Richard Riso on the different 'levels' we see in the Enneagram. Riso created a detailed analysis of each of the 9

Enneagram types, where he subdivided each type into 3 levels, labelling these Healthy, Average or Unhealthy.[13] As an Enneagram 4, I found this fascinating and very recognizable in my own life across different seasons! But the gold is not necessarily just in his interpretation of the Enneagram, it is the connection established between how we show up in the world and how fulfilled we are. It's not that *people* are intrinsically labelled as Healthy, Average, or Unhealthy. For all of us, this is a sliding scale. In some seasons of life, we are basically our worst selves. Spiteful, selfish, turned in on ourselves, quick to see the worst in ourselves and in others. And yet, we all possess the capacity to transcend our worst self and reflect love and light into the world as our best self. And—news flash—although I doubt this will be a huge surprise—you can tell how the tree is doing by looking at the fruit.

The biggest determining factor to the 'level' you show up as comes down to one thing—guess what?—how much fulfillment we experience in our day-to-day lives. When we resonate with our highest *Healthy* levels of fulfillment, we exude magic into the world and feel a deep sense of purpose and belonging. We contribute to society in positive ways and enrich the lives of others. We feel seen and our giftedness has the resonance of being acknowledged by others. When we deteriorate to the lowest *Unhealthy* levels, utter destructive chaos descends, resulting in toxic behavior, and even addiction and total self-destruction. We lose sight of any meaning or purpose and everything feels futile.

Doesn't that make it insane that this is something we very rarely talk about and pay very little attention to as we go about our daily lives? We might ask *"How are you?"* in social situations, but when's the last time you asked a friend *"How fulfilled are you feeling today?"*. And more than that, when's the last time you asked yourself this same question?!

We go through some seasons where we feel strong connection to our values, and we are satisfied and exhilarated by the opportunities all around us. When you're in high fulfillment, your energy flows and it can feel like everything you touch turns to gold. But in other seasons we get stuck in low fulfillment. Maybe back in your corporate days you hated your job, or you didn't get on with your boss or a co-worker. Maybe now you're in business, all your clients feel like nightmare clients, which leaves you constantly questioning whether you are making an impact in the world or are any good at anything. Maybe you feel like a failure, or that you don't have the approval of people you care about. Maybe you're aware that other people really push your buttons, and it's frustrating to see them succeed while you feel like you're struggling. Life feels futile when you can't connect with any deeper meaning or purpose in your day-to-day life. You can tell how the tree is doing by looking at the fruit.

Can you see that fulfillment is an important concept for us to embrace, but more that that—it's our rope ladder to exit and escape when we are in a dark season. Instead of labelling ourselves as terrible, bad, unlovable people who are too much, we need to look at our too-much-ness through this lens of fulfillment, and instead ask ourselves, *how fulfilled am I in this current season? Am I putting myself in the right places? Am I surrounded by the right people?*

And there is also an important distinction I want to make at this stage, because it plays on our deepest fears as women who feel like too much.

The Best Self Version vs the Evil Twin Version of Too Much

So far, I've talked about too much in positive terms. And that's important because it is great to be gifted. It is great to be special. It is great to be too much for people's narrow definition of what and who you are allowed to be. It is good to push on those boundaries and find your life's fulfillment through not denying your gifts—this is us channelling our too-much-ness into showing up as our best selves, or the 'Best Self version of too much'. It's the fruit of feeling like we are in high fulfillment. But there is also another version of too much that I call 'the evil twin version of too much'. This kind of too-much-ness happens when we haven't yet put the pieces together about where the problem truly lies. We feel like too much, and we feel like where we are is not enough. And this hurts. But we can't yet see how much power we have to resolve this ourselves, so we get tangled up in the way we try to fix it.

You've probably had the experience of finding another person to be too much before, and it's true, as much as we know the pain of being made to feel like too much, we also sometimes feel that certain people in our lives want and need more from us than we have to give. You know, the kind of emotional vampire who only wants to talk about themselves or vent endlessly about their problems with no intention of heeding any constructive solutions. And for those of us who feel like too much, this can feel deeply uncomfortable because how can we label *our* too-much-ness in positive terms, when here is the evidence that this person who *I* feel to be too much doesn't impact positively—and in fact, it's a nightmare to get sucked into their vortex?

Here's the thing—'too much' has two different faces, and with practice, we can choose which of them we show up as. I know I have had seasons as an adult where I felt extremely lonely and like I was struggling to feel like I belonged or really fit. I was hurting and really just wanted to make the pain I was feeling stop. Honestly, I feel kind of embarrassed when I look back on seasons where I was the evil twin version of too much! But I think all of us who are human, and especially those of us who are telling ourselves a negative story about what it means to be too much, will have slipped into this mode at some points in our lives. But there's an important difference between the Best Self version of too much and the Evil Twin version, that helps us tell the difference and make a correction if we need to.

The Best Self version comes from being our natural, sparky selves. It's almost an overabundance of exuberant energy. It can be overwhelming for others, but it isn't manipulative or competitive. It is just us exercising our gifts instead of hiding them away. Whereas the draining kind of too-much-ness, the Evil Twin version, is when we are acting this out in ways that aren't emotionally healthy for us and aren't helpful for other people.

Have you ever found yourself talking so much it's like you can't stop, and you can tell that the people listening are finding it a bit intense but there is suddenly this impulse within you—"*I don't care. I have to finish saying this even if they don't feel like hearing it. I need someone to hear me say this and I don't care who*". In this moment, your need to express yourself or have a social interaction outweighs the needs of the person you are speaking to. You have an unmet need—maybe loneliness, boredom, lack of stimulation, which are really common for entrepreneurs as we often work alone for much of the week, or just keeping a lifetime of emotional bruises squashed down for too long—and you're determined that in this moment, the person you're speaking to is going to meet that need.

To put it another way, you're struggling in some way and not feeling good about yourself. And instead of taking a step back and making a decision about how to respond to your unmet need, you end up projecting it onto someone else and making it their problem. "*Well sorry,*" we say internally (and by the way we're absolutely not sorry in this situation), "*but I was made to feel insignificant and like I wasn't worth listening to as a child, which doesn't make me feel good about myself, so now I'm going to make sure you listen to my very long and rambling story because my need to feel validated and heard outweighs your needs in this moment."*

There can be many triggers for this kind of behavior. Maybe you're having a hard time in your business, or a particular client is making unreasonable demands. Or we feel that we can't express ourselves without judgement. Often it's because there is a boundary we need to put up in a certain situation and we don't know how, so we do nothing and vent it out on someone else because it's easier to just blame someone else than face it head on. And it's Evil Twin behavior because it sucks the air out of the room.

But when we apply our knowledge of high and low fulfillment to this kind of scenario—it changes everything. What we actually need in this moment is to find greater fulfillment—to recognize that we are sinking into a low level of fulfillment and the fruit of that is toxic behavior that further isolates us from others. We don't need to vent or tear others down to make ourselves feel better, we need to increase our sense of fulfillment so that we can ascend to a high level of fulfillment again and show up as the Best Self version of too much. This could look like finding ways to express ourselves and be heard in positive ways. It could be taking on a new responsibility or hobby where we make new friendships and widen our social circle. It could be taking decisive action about a hard situation we're struggling with and putting some better boundaries in place, or it could be practicing better self care.

But when we're in Evil Twin mode we don't usually feel confident to find a positive solution—because remember, we've shifted into low fulfillment and we're feeling powerless. So we make it someone else's problem and require them to make up the deficit we feel. We are hurting, but instead of owning that and meeting our emotional needs, we make demands of others in the hope that this will make it hurt less. We are basically requiring them to make up for the dissonance we feel. And although it feels like we need other people to save us, the actual cause of our pain and discouragement in these moments isn't our too-much-ness, it's our lack of fulfillment. It's something that only you can do something about. And needing someone—a spouse, friend, therapist, or even a stranger in the street—to rescue us as if we are some helpless martyr is a huge clue that we're slipping into Evil Twin too-much-ness.

Here's what we need to remember—the Evil Twin version of too much may look like you, but it isn't you. And when we show up as the Evil Twin version of too much, what we need isn't a personality transplant or self-recrimination, or a savior to rescue us—it's greater fulfillment. It's a moment where we can say, "*Wait, I think this feeling/behavior is the Evil Twin version of too much showing up! This means something about this situation is making me feel a low level of fulfillment. I wonder what that is?*" And we can know that this is a moment of opportunity. We can shift our feeling of powerLESSness to powerFULness. This is often where the WHERE of our current situation becomes significant. We have to stop putting ourselves in the wrong places and allowing ourselves to stay unfulfilled.

Remember the second part of our mantra—*It means THIS is not enough.* So if you're working for a nightmare client in your consulting business, it's time to take action because there IS a solution and it is probably way simpler than you're expecting. Sign a better client and fire the nightmare one. *Struggling to get on with a difficult family member?* Put boundaries in place that help you feel safe. *Stuck in a romantic relationship that has gone toxic and doesn't meet your needs?* Believe there is something better out there for you and trust yourself to go and find it.

When you realize your Evil Twin version is activated, show her compassion and acceptance. It doesn't mean you're a toxic person, it means you're in low fulfillment. It's ultimately about asking yourself, *what do I need in this moment and why do I feel like I'm not getting it? What am I making someone else responsible for? Why do I feel so unfulfilled and frustrated in this situation?* I promise you, taking responsibility for meeting your needs *yourself* will create greater fulfillment. Because, ultimately, you are responsible for your life. You are responsible for living a life that fulfills you and makes sense of your gifts. Life can be short. You can either bleed all over people—and I spent years doing this—or you can be in command of how you show up. When we drift into the Evil Twin version of too much, we are trying to farm out that responsibility that only we can carry, to other people. And that's not going to serve us, or them.

Doing Life from the Overflow

Want to know something pretty cool? Although it feels awful to realize we have showed up as the Evil Twin version, there is an upside to developing this self awareness. It means we can grow and change, and choose something better.

When we feel more fulfilled, we are more able to meet our own needs and develop strong inner resources that shift our Evil Twin version to Best Self version. And when we are operating from a place of empowerment and abundance, we don't just meet our *own* needs, we have more energy left over to help other people.

We can use this overflow to give out to others, rather than needing to hoard every scrap of energy that comes our way to deal with our difficult emotions. Can you see how powerful this is? If we channel our too-much-ness into fulfillment rather than despondency—we can choose to show up as the Best Self, not the Evil Twin. We don't need to be emotional 'takers', we can instead ground ourselves and meet our own needs when difficult emotions show up. And then our relationships aren't just about taking from other people, or forcing them to accommodate us. We can be present and available for two-way communication and easy interactions. You know, laughing, and fun experiences and things. Genuine connection, instead of just waiting for them to pause so we can resume venting again.

Understanding fulfillment, and how we are doing with it, is quite literally, transformational. It's because fulfillment is the path to discovering the 'more' that will make your too-much-ness feel like just the right amount. Can you see why it makes a great lens for us to be looking through as we explore how and why we feel like too much?

Now you may be reading this and feeling all kinds of shame for having been the Evil Twin version of too much at times in your life. But you don't need to get hung up on it, even though it might feel uncomfortable to face it head on. All of us show up as the Evil Twin version at times, and it's my belief that we can forgive ourselves for not doing better when we didn't know better. The same is true if you fall back into Evil Twin behavior from time to time. Now you know better, you are equipped to do better—it's not about forcing other people to meet your emotional needs, it's about identifying and seeking out your own fulfillment.

And let's not forget that most people in the world don't know how to understand these things about themselves, and don't develop the self-awareness that means they can choose to respond instead of defaulting to reacting when hard emotions come up. No one is born knowing these things, and most people are doing their best with what they have.

I also want to clarify here that I don't mean we should never ask for help or speak to others about how we are feeling. Most women entrepreneurs are fiercely independent and actually need to work on breaking their staunch self-reliance by allowing others to be involved in their lives and businesses. It's not that you shouldn't ask for help in doing this work—it's that you should do the work and not try to circumvent the big emotions you are feeling by resorting to Evil

Twin behavior. A lot of these things would be excellent to work on with a trained therapist, because what I'm referring to with Evil Twin behavior is moving away from entangled co-dependency and toxic behaviors, and instead knowing we can help ourselves feel better by dealing with the matter internally first. We will talk more about this in Chapter 3!

So—we've covered a lot of ground in these first couple of chapters, and we've built the foundation for everything we will explore throughout the rest of this book. The one thing I would love you to take away at this stage is this powerful mantra. Say it with me, because we're going to be coming back to this again and again.

When I feel like too much. It means THIS is not enough. Which means I need to look for more.

Again:

When I feel like too much. It means THIS is not enough. Which means I need to look for more.

Don't worry if it's not embedded yet. We are really just getting started with this new paradigm. Whenever we do mindset work, we are creating new pathways in our brains, and thinking things we have never thought before. So, we can't just jump into something totally new: we need to create the pathway first. Our brains like predictability. They have established thought pathways and when we think about things we commonly think about, our brains go, *"Oh! I know this pathway!"* And will follow it, exactly the same. Thought A leads to Thought B leads to Thought C in a perfect sequence.

So, one of the things that makes mindset work feel challenging is because you are thinking thoughts your brain doesn't know how to hold. It's like pushing your brain into the middle of a forest it has never been to before, with no discernible paths to follow and expecting it to know what to do. When we are creating new pathways, we are thinking thoughts we have never thought before. So, we can't just be like, *"Ok brain, find the path!"* There IS no path. It hasn't been formed yet. And the process of forming a path in nature takes years—decades, and even centuries. But luckily for us, our brains are way more elastic than this and we can make amazing progress with mindset work QUICKLY. We need to help our brains learn the right way to go. We need mantras and intentional phrases that we can use to guide the way while the new pathways get created. So, this is why we're going to keep coming back to this new intentional thought pathway, and we're going to embed it so that your brain can learn to make it into a 'no brainer', if you will.

When I feel like too much. It means THIS is not enough. Which means I need to look for more.

But what does it actually mean to 'look for more'? I'm glad you asked, because that's what we're jumping straight into in Chapter 3. I'll see you there!

CHAPTER 2 SUMMARY

- It All Comes Down to Fulfillment
- The Best Self Version vs the Evil Twin Version of Too Much
- Doing Life From the Overflow

3 You Need to Look For More

In the last chapter I shared a mantra to help you navigate your journey out of too-much-ness and into looking for more:

> ***When I feel like too much. It means THIS is not enough. Which means I need to look for more.***

We've looked at what it means to be too much, and why it's time to re-imagine that label and see it for the gift it truly is and the magical things it says about you. But what does it really mean to be looking for more? Where do we look? And what is 'more', and how can we know when we have found it? In this chapter we have an important shift to explore—moving from external to internal. And we will examine this in the way we see ourselves, the way we relate to others and the way we approach business. I'll also be introducing you to a pair of 'magical cousins' that will transform the way you hold your too-much-ness, and begin to soothe the turbulence it causes us without dulling your drive or ambition.

Stop Looking Outward, Learn to Look Inward

The first thing I want to establish is that we find our 'more', not by looking outward, but by looking inward. It is uncomfortable to realize you've been living in the land of 'not enough' and it can feel like opening a drawer so full of junk we aren't sure we'll be able to close it again.

For many of us, we have done the bulk of our lives to this point based on an assumption of '*who I am supposed to be*'. We smile. We get the grades. We get the promotions. And yet… We aren't fulfilled. And if you are reading this book, and you have done your best to be successful in your education, your career, and now your consulting business, I'm imagining that you have put in a considerable amount of energy trying to fit inside the lines and be like other people. But it doesn't work, because you are going through your days feeling like you're too much. You aren't feeling fulfilled. You don't fit inside the lines. You don't feel like you've found the place you fit.

Ready for a truth bomb?

It's time to stop taking your cues from other people. To stop being only who our parents told us to be, or who our boss needed us to be, or who our friends decided *they* would be. It's time to show up as your authentic self. But now the drawer is open and who even is she? And why does it feel like it's such a hard question to answer?

After my burnout episode, the only thing I did for around 7 months was go to therapy once a week, rest in bed, and on account of us not being able to afford many TV channels in those days, watch a ridiculous number of daytime TV documentaries. To this day, I know some really random stuff about becoming a West End Singer, rehab after prison (!), and marine wildlife that likes to eat other marine wildlife, because of the many, many documentaries I watched in those seven months. But guess what.

During that phase when all I really did was go to therapy, my therapist would ask me, each week, "*How are you?*" And I would say, "*Fine.*" And she would give me that look that all therapists and coaches have perfected, you know, the quizzical side eye. The raised eyebrow look of "*Really?*" Because obviously, I wasn't fine. My life had fallen apart. I wasn't working. I wasn't socializing. I didn't have anything going on at all except ill health and fatigue. But I didn't have any words to describe what I was feeling, because I felt nothing. I was totally dissociated from my body because that had been my survival technique in dealing with my chronic health issues in the probably 5 years before I hit burnout. But because I was dissociated, I had no answer to "how are you?" because I had switched off my emotions and body responses and was in a state of perpetual numbness.

And it is ok to realize that this is where you are, even today, as you read this book. This is where most people spend most of their lives, because life can be messy and devastatingly painful. Human beings feel deep emotions—especially those of us who feel like too much, because you know, we're too much! But we might not understand our deep emotions and often we don't enjoy them. We fear that if we allow them, they will overwhelm us or worse, stay with us in full intensity forever. It makes perfect sense to switch off from this and do everything we can to NOT feel. And that numbing process protects us for a while. But to discover what your 'more' looks like, you need to reconnect with your body and reconnect with your authentic self.

I speak to women all the time who don't feel any excitement about their business or life plans, and don't feel like they particularly care about anything in front of them. They are constantly pulling against their intuition. And this is the crazy part—we so often know exactly what to do, but because we don't trust ourselves we act like we need someone to tell us what to do. In effect, we block the phone number of our intuition, and then we wonder why we feel so dissatisfied and unfulfilled.

Because the honest truth is, we get so used to just showing up as who people need us to be. We smile and fawn. We pretend to share interests because small talk is less threatening than voicing an opinion or risking offending someone. We take our cues from social media trends and buy stuff we don't particularly need or ever use. And to break this pattern, we need to switch ourselves back on.

When I was a teenager, I was incredibly bold and never doubted I could do the things I wanted to do. And sometimes I wonder, when did that change? As I mentioned in Chapter 1, I started a rock band with two of my best friends from school when we were 14. By the time we were 16, we had recorded a demo tape and sent it in the mail to rock venues and promoters up and down the country. As a result, we played gigs all across the UK, and we got the interest of a major recording studio who brought us in to record a proper EP. Even though ultimately it never went any further than this, it never occurred to me we couldn't do it. When I was 20, I started writing a novel in my bedroom at home, and again, I never finished it, but I wasn't put off from starting it out of a fear that I wouldn't be able to do it. But then somewhere along the line, I lost that ability to be bold and brave. I toned things down and showed more caution. I quit my band to do the responsible thing and go to college and after that, got a 'proper' corporate career job. I don't regret that decision—the band had run its course and I was ready for a bigger challenge and at the time, going to college was my 'more'. But my burnout episode at 27 was absolutely a turning point for me, because I stopped believing it was a good thing to go big or go home.

I think a lot of us have had similar experiences. We are unafraid to be our authentic selves in our early lives. Think about how bold children are at the age of four, or nine. But then something happens to cast doubt on all that confidence, and it all changes. Maybe you've had a similar experience to me in going through burnout and being forced to question: *wait, who am I, if I can't do all the things I want? Who am I when I have to factor in chronic health issues that mean I don't recognize the person I am now?* Or maybe you've had a series of setbacks, disappointments, or rejection. People we've trusted can let us down. Relationships can fail. A promising career implodes into a messy end. We come face to face with our health limitations. People we care about don't make it to middle age. And I honestly believe that this is why a lot of us end up in too-small lives where we feel like we're too much. We get our fingers burned in all kinds of ways, and we don't want to take the same risks again, so we settle for less so that everything can go back to feeling safe. More than this, we don't even realize we are doing it.

The Breadcrumb Trail Leading to Your 'More'

When I started my business 10 years ago, can you guess what my first year revenue goal was? This might be a surprise, but it was... $6,000. We had a small gap in our family finances, and it was my job to fill that gap. When I look back on that now, I don't recognize that version of myself. But it is also extremely understandable that after everything I went through in my burnout episode and the loss of my career, I didn't want big and bold any more. I wanted safety. And so, I played it safe in almost every part of my life. Over the last 10 years of my business, I can absolutely see now that I have been walking the slow path of reconnecting with my authentic self. The one who believes she can do pretty much anything, even with some energy limitations to take account of. The one who loves to play electric guitar and record music in a home studio, who has crazy hair colors, who travels the world, and who takes big swings. It has been a process of finding the threads of the person I once allowed myself to be, and like a 1920s telephone operator connecting calls, plugging the wires back in, one by one. And I wonder—what threads of your past self are waiting for you to rediscover them?

When I do transformational coaching with my clients, we do the work of setting powerful revenue goals. This can feel really difficult if you cannot immediately access your authentic self. But here's the thing I've noticed. As we create the blueprint for your seven figure consulting business and the legacy life that this enables, your authentic self starts to reappear. This is such a rewarding path to follow, because it enables you to hear your intuitive voice and take actions that are in alignment with your mind and body.

If this feels hard or out of reach for you at the moment, try asking yourself, *"Who am I when no one is watching?"*. Maybe you have a few niche hobbies or that guilty pleasure TV show that you've never admitted to watching. It's also worth getting curious— where are the areas of your life that you find yourself saying words you are indifferent to, about stuff you know deep down you don't actually care about, expressing opinions you don't actually have, but kind of feel like you should? Who were you when you were young, and the world hadn't taught you to hide? What were you passionate about? What clothes did you wear? What gifts did you have? What threads can you find that tailed off, maybe several decades ago, and might be there, just waiting for you to find them and weave them back in? When we can truly understand this about ourselves and start to see what we like and what we want, it can give us vital clues about what we are actually looking for in business and in life. It starts to reveal our 'more'.

One of the things that is my 'more' is deep connection. I don't know about you, but I have always been looking for more than basic. I've always wanted to do life on a deeper level. Don't tell me you're fine. I want to know everything—*how are you, really? How are you feeling? What did you have for breakfast? What insane things are going on in your life? How is your healing journey going? What are you working towards and feeling super good about at the moment?* I have always wanted deeper friendships and a deeper married relationship. Surface level niceness just doesn't cut it for me. I don't want a *"Hi...Bye..."* acquaintance level friendship. I'm not interested in faking it, or putting on a performance, or making everything look Insta-perfect. I have often got in trouble by being too honest, and too vulnerable. I've always been looking for more, even when I didn't know I was looking for more. And maybe you feel the same way. Or maybe your 'more' is something else. More freedom. More space. More experiences. More money. More people. More influence. More fine dining. More cozy living. The sky is the limit and it can look like whatever you want it to!

When we can reconnect with our authentic self and start to reattach the threads that make us who we are, everything changes. We see the world differently. And we are shifting from a world where we can only say no to ourselves, to a world where we understand what we want to be saying yes to. I am convinced that reconnecting with your authentic self is essential when it comes to finding your 'more' and building the seven figure business that makes your too-muchness feel like just the right amount. And this can only happen when we stop looking outward to what everyone else wants from us and for us, and instead we learn to look inward.

Radical Self Improvement and Its Magical Cousin

An important part of discovering our 'more' and saying yes to ourselves is sensing what it would look like to be your best self and starting to consciously step into this. I call this Radical Self Improvement and (probably not a surprise) it's something I am obsessed with. I suspect the same may be true for you as a high achiever. Why? Because we experience deep fulfillment when we are free to show up as our best selves without dumbing down—and as you'll remember from Chapter 2, this matters because fulfillment is the path that leads to our destination of 'more'. The work of becoming your best self is a worthy life goal. And more than that, when you show up in the world with love and light, this not only benefits others—it inspires them to do the same.

I believe we are all given a purpose and a path in the world, and our job is to discern it and follow it. As high-achievers, this is often wired into us. We crave excellence and achievement. It's not that we just want to be better than everyone else. Even when we are only in competition with ourselves, we want to win because there is something thrilling about exceeding our limits and we get a lot of satisfaction from seeing things done to an exceptional standard. And if you are in a season where you might be tempted to show up as the Evil Twin version of too much, this could absolutely manifest as being cutthroat and aggressively competitive and needing to win at all costs. But there is another path that is always open to us, that of 'collaboration over competition.' Achieving excellence ourselves is great. But achieving it AND seeing others also becoming the best they can be? Even better. Let's all shine!

But as you'll know, as a fellow high-achiever, there can be a darker side to Radical Self Improvement. We love to push ourselves and achieve. We love to be productive and get a million things done in a day. We love to say yes to everything and be the person who makes it happen. But it goes wrong when we drive ourselves to do all this by force and self-discipline. Because, guess what happens? Burnout and exhaustion. I know for me, I have this inner drill sergeant who can be like, *"Come on, Jessica! Do your workout! Make sure you do the agility training with the dog! Eat nutritious food! Be the best coach you can be! Read mind improving books with the kids! Did you journal today?!"* And this barked list of orders continues all day every day, if I let it.

I love layers. I love optimization. I love to go through my daily life and perfect my routine from the perspective of timing, health, efficiency, and all kinds of metrics. The length of my morning walk, the food I eat for breakfast, my beauty routines, my practices for a good mindset, the clothes I wear.

This absolutely has its roots in how I have recovered from chronic health issues, and dealt with seasons of low energy and fatigue. But it's also wired into me. I love to find the best options and rinse and repeat, always optimizing and improving. But, at times, this can mean that life gets very complicated. I can't tell you how many shampoos and conditioners I have in the shower. At one point, I noticed I was using five different hair serums! And you might not want to sit next to me on a plane because I have a little travel sack that may as well be a Mary Poppins bag—I have everything I need for the flight—and I mean EVERYTHING—in miniature form from lip balm to charger cables to healthy snacks. But because I love to create layers, it means that I often create a very heavy load for myself, and then my inner drill sergeant turns up to make sure I don't stop trying to lift it all. And this is where it really helps to understand that Radical Self Improvement by itself isn't enough. We also need to pair it with its magical cousin, Radical Self Acceptance.

Radical Self Acceptance is the nurturing part of you that doesn't need you to be different or more. Radical Self Acceptance is about seeing and acknowledging the value you already have. The things you like about yourself. The things you have already achieved and overcome. The things you are proud of yourself for. It's switching the dial from self criticism to self love.

Why are Radical Self Improvement and Radical Self Acceptance cousins and not twins? This is because they go well together but there is also a healthy tension between them. Radical Self Improvement means we are always noticing the ways that we can take the next step towards our best self. But Radical Self Acceptance means that we can also validate and enjoy the version of us that we are without those things. It's a small thing but it makes a world of difference. Without

Radical Self Acceptance, we push and berate ourselves and never slow down. But without Radical Self Improvement, we end up stuck without an outlet for our drive and ambition. Radical Self Improvement pushes us to stretch towards 'more'. Radical Self Acceptance means we can be gentle with ourselves on the journey and allow stops to rest!

I often think of Radical Self Acceptance as the 'easiest hardest' thing. What I mean is—it is so simple to just let go of all our 'shoulds' and choose gratitude and acceptance. But it also goes against every fiber of our beings as high-achievers, who kind of always want to be given a score out of 100 or an A-grade. And this often comes out in my work with women consultants when they realize that they've been trying to build their consulting business according to a list of someone else's rules and priorities, and that doing business actually isn't about working insanely hard to win the prize. A key part of getting to seven figures with ease is uncovering the ways of doing business that are super strategic AND ALSO feel really good to you. Then you build your strategy around those things. It's so simple. But it's really uncomfortable to unlearn all of the internal rules we have that tell us it has to be hard. Radical Self Acceptance IS deeply uncomfortable, but it is also wonderfully freeing to stop being in constant motion always striving, and to simply just be. And one of the most valuable tools we can give ourselves when it comes to Radical Self Acceptance, is the ability to stop looking for external validation and switch it for internal validation.

The Great Exchange—Switching External Validation for Internal Validation

If you feel dissociated from your body and out of touch with your authentic self, it can feel like external validation is all there is. Maybe you can relate—when we are geared towards external validation to make us feel safe and, well, validated, it's a lot of work. We need other people to agree with us otherwise it feels like we're not impressive enough. We need external things such as money, a successful business, a nice house, a nice car and expensive clothes to make us feel like we're worth anything. We need to be the center of attention at all times, otherwise it feels like we might crumple into a heap without other people constantly endorsing how special and valued we are. And often, we need to feel like we're the best in the room, and we work this out by constantly ranking and comparing ourselves to others. Sounds familiar, doesn't it? Because craving external validation is another manifestation of the Evil Twin version of too much. *"Tell me I'm the best so I don't get swallowed up by my overwhelming feelings of inadequacy!"*—needing things and people to plug the void of the unfulfillment we feel.

And not only is it exhausting to the people around us, who we are making responsible for our sense of personal wellbeing, it is staggeringly unsatisfying to us. The good opinion of others is another dopamine hit that, just like the empty 'vanity likes' on social media, feels great for three seconds and then vanishes. When we feel like we NEED the approval of others in order to function as a person, we feel fragile and fraught because we are literally giving away the power that should only belong to us. More than this, we can actually find that our focus on Radical Self Improvement without its magical cousin, Radical Self Acceptance, can leave us focusing solely on what we AREN'T. This can exacerbate the fear we've already discussed that many of us who are too much experience—the fear that we are not enough. The combination of the drive for Radical Self Improvement mixed in with an unhealthy dose of the desire for external validation and the fear that we are not enough is a toxic cocktail. But there is a powerful antidote. Remembering to add Radical Self Acceptance back in to temper our drive for high achievement in ourselves.

Because when we practice Radical Self Acceptance, we ARE giving ourselves internal validation.

This is why it feels so good to free ourselves from the shackles of external validation—by discovering what it means to be able to give ourselves the gift of *in*ternal validation. I often describe this in my workshops as being able to visualize your inner 'intrinsic' value as a column of light filled with silver sparkles. I love to visualize this as something located in the center of my chest, almost like a powerful lava lamp that is switched on all the time. Everything you are good at. Everything you are passionate about. Everything about you that lights you up and radiates out to other people. Everything that makes you special. Everything you do, say and are that connects with other people and creates resonance. It is there on the days when we feel like we're knocking the ball out of the park, winning new contracts, delivering spectacular results for our clients, reaping the rewards that come from having established a good reputation in our field. And, believe it or not, your intrinsic value and validation is still there on the crappy days, when a promising sale has fallen through, when a client doesn't like our big ideas, or when we realize there was a mistake in an important proposal that is going to cost us money to fix.

When you can root yourself in your intrinsic value, your internal validation, you are finally free to play the game of business without your whole value as a person on the table. It means you can take chances in business because you are the same amazing person whether the deal comes off or not. It means you can feel good about yourself even after a bad day at work. And it is a really important piece of the puzzle when it comes to looking for your 'more,' because it means that you aren't growing your business to seven figures to prove yourself or to show that you have value. It means you are free to soar, because whatever happens today or this month or this year, you already won.

And more than that, when we are secure because our validation comes from our internal value rather than external things, we can show up differently in life. We can show up as our authentic self and let people know who we really are, and how we feel about things. We can love and accept ourselves and not constantly be running through a laundry list of the things we need to change about our appearance, character, lifestyle. We can attract the opportunities, friendships, even the romantic partner of our dreams because we are at peace with ourselves. We can choose to love and to be of service instead of just needing people and things to fill the desperate void in our souls from all the things we fear deep down we are not.

When people say *"you are enough"*, this is what they are referring to. Because you ARE enough. When we fear that we are not enough, it's the easiest thing in the world to lean into Radical Self Improvement to try and plug the gap. But that is another way of perpetuating the cycle of looking for external validation. When we practise Radical Self Acceptance we are leaning into interval validation. And it radically changes how we try and achieve our goals. You can be at peace with yourself. It means you are free to soar and achieve your peak fulfillment through your seven figure business instead of needing to achieve seven figures in revenue because you are desperate to be someone different to who you were made to be—your authentic and best self. And when we really nail this—everything feels different in life and business.

Starting to Envision Your 'More'

When we allow Radical Self Acceptance instead of just powering forward on hyper-speed with Radical Self Improvement, we create a safe space to explore what feels like it's calling to you. One of my favorite things about the work I do is starting to clear the path for my clients to connect with their peak fulfillment in life—their 'more.' I speak to women all the time who are successful consultancy owners, and on paper they have everything they set out to build. But there's a spark of an idea for something deeper.

I remember one of my clients, Rosalyn, was crushing it as a consultant. She was in demand. She had built up an impressive client portfolio and she was building out her consulting team and creating capacity so she could expand her reach and help more companies. Her revenue had doubled while we were working together. But one day, when we were in the middle of a coaching session, she paused, mid-sentence. Then she said, *"Jessica, I just feel like there's more I want to do than this."* And at the time, it really took me by surprise. But, being a coach, my job is to get curious so I asked her, *"Ok. So what more is there?"* She paused again and said in a firmer voice, *"I want to create a leadership movement for women. I want to support them in their careers and use everything I've learned in my corporate career to give back and help other women."*

She even knew where she would host retreats for these women, and had a semi-plan already mapped out in her head of how the logistics would work. And the magical thing in that moment was it totally made sense. It wasn't crazy or out of reach—it was her next level. Right now you may have a spark of an idea. You may simply have a feeling that you were made for more, with none of the details worked out. It may be close to fully formed or it may need to 'cook' for a while longer. You may have a structured vision and a corresponding business plan, or it may just be that feeling we get sometimes that something we can't yet put into words is just around the corner.

Remember our mantra:

> ***When I feel like too much. It means THIS is not enough. Which means I need to look for more.***

If you have the gift of being too much, it's not for nothing. It is for something. It is for a purpose. There is a 'more' out there that is waiting for you to find it. Getting clarity on this and what it looks like is your life's work, but we have a ton of time to think about this together while you are reading this book. That clarity, when it comes, is a whole other gift all by itself. Now you have two gifts—the gift of being too much, AND the gift of understanding how to use it. How lucky is that?! But before you are ready to start on your journey of looking for your 'more,' there's a step we can't afford to skip over.

Writing Your Permission Slip

Here's something you may not have considered before. You are allowed to be too much. We can spend so much time trying to be less, wishing we were different, pretending we are fine with fine. Resigning ourselves to the feeling that we may never fit or have what we want. But that's a story you can stop telling yourself right now. Consider this your permission slip from me—you are allowed to be too much. You are allowed to fully embrace your authentic self. Yes, really. You are allowed to find your old life not enough. You are allowed to want more. You are allowed to go on the journey of looking for more. Maybe you've heard people say *'If I'm too much, you're welcome to go and find less'*. Going by that logic, it follows that if they can go and look for less, we also need to raise the bar on ourselves and look for more.

But the thing is, I can give you the permission slip but you need to fill it out and sign it. Are you willing to begin the journey of looking for your 'more'? It is something that only you can define and embark upon. And this is important because one of the things you might get super aware of as you start to connect with your authentic self and explore what your 'more' looks like, is that there may be people in your life who love you but do not want you to change. Most of us find the concept of change uncomfortable and sometimes we find it terrifying. And when you start to switch your old, fixed mindset for a growth mindset and start to step into your best, authentic self, it can make things feel really weird.

My family thought I was insane when I set up my coaching business ten years ago. And even on my business journey I have had the experience many times of having a really lovely group of entrepreneur friends, but suddenly having this feeling that I'm being called to something beyond where we've all got to. And the realization that in order to stay true to my own fulfillment, I'm not ready to put down roots yet because I need to pull ahead of the pack and stretch towards my 'more'.

I don't know if you've ever had the experience of going to a networking event for women entrepreneurs and saying you plan to grow your business to seven figures. In a lot of rooms, it's a record-scratch moment. Because when we get clarity about who we truly are and what we are planning to grow towards, it is often the case that the people around us don't want to come on the journey too. People who we thought of as friends are triggered by our expansiveness. Relationships change as we start working a lot less and earning a lot more. Entrepreneurship is very often a path of one. There are absolutely seasons where we have lots of friends and companions on the road. But we need to make our peace with being on the path of one. As an adult, you are responsible for your life and how you use it. You are responsible for whether you reach High fulfillment, coast in Average fulfillment or spiral down to Low fulfillment.

We can't control other people's lives, their choices, or their emotions. And they can't expect to control ours. You are only responsible for *your* choices and *your* emotions. It doesn't make sense to NOT follow the path to your 'more' out of fear that you might upset other people, because in all likelihood they won't be appeased if you decide not to. And then nobody wins, because life can be short and we don't get a do-over. The person who needs to sign your permission slip is you.

And if you're reading this, and feeling a sense of grief come up as you think about your old life and the parts of it you felt tied to, even if that was a love-hate relationship where you were frustrated by your reality and desperate to move past it, but also find yourself reticent to move onto 'more'—know that this is totally normal. With every uplevel we make on the road of personal and business growth, as we are welcoming in the new version of us—which I like to call your Next Level Self—we are also saying goodbye to our old version. And if grief comes up, it is important to embrace it, even when it is triggered at the most unexpected moments.

A few years ago, I had just returned from the first international retreat I had ever been to. Everything about it was an uplevel. I travelled by myself for the first time in my life. I was still shaking off some residual social anxiety after the pandemic lockdown era and it was hard to be in a room with people. It meant leaving my husband and kids at home on the other side of the Atlantic Ocean. But it was also a powerful permission slip. I had never really had the budget to travel in my business before, and I didn't feel like it was something I was even allowed to do. But I did it and I'm so glad that I did.

When I got home, I realized that there were some things in my old life before the retreat that just didn't fit any more. The first thing that had to go? My robe. It might sound crazy, but as I unpacked my things after the retreat, I looked at my sad, worn-out robe hanging on the back of my bedroom door and realized: *"That just does not fit who I am any more."* I had had the same robe for 20 years and it had been with me through college, my corporate days, my life pre-kids when I was really unwell with chronic illness, my life immediately post-kids when I was struggling to adapt to life as a new mom, the phase of life where my dad was dying—and then the phase where he did die—of cancer. This robe was a symbol of all the struggle, all the sickness, all the hard times. And suddenly, I just had to get rid of it. I was ready for a new story.

But as I folded it and put it in a bag for goodwill, I felt a lump in my throat. In saying goodbye to my sad little robe, I was drawing a line between my old life and my Next Level life. And part of me was scared to let go, crazy as that may sound. What if I lost myself by letting go of that old version of me? What if that was dishonoring the things *she* went through and the hardships she had faced? I was literally giving away my comfort blanket from those years. But I also knew I was ready to make that commitment to myself. I *can* let go of the past because I don't need it any more. I can clear space for something new. I can clear space for something better. I did in fact buy a new robe shortly afterwards and, even now when I wear it every morning, I am still reminded that in that moment I let go of my old self and stepped into my Next Level Self. And I can continue to do that with whatever comes up to be released, again and again.

If you're reading this and you know only too well how hard it can feel to let go of your old self, even though you also know that you're ready and it's time, allow yourself to grieve. It is incredibly poignant to acknowledge all the hurt that our past selves have experienced. The shame. The disappointments. The things we hoped would work out that didn't, and the pain we experienced in the fall out. It is also normal for that feeling to spike when we come to the point of severing those ties. But—when it comes to saying goodbye to our old selves—we're ready to let go. It does us good to let go of the things that no longer fit. It might be closing down parts of your business that used to be aligned but you have now grown out of, or letting go of legacy clients, or even legacy team members, or making material changes in your clothing, cars, houses, remodels. Maybe there are people in your life that you're aware cannot come with you on this journey because they don't get it and they don't want you to grow. They like the old version of you, and don't understand why you need to look for your 'more'.

Remember our mantra:

When I feel like too much. It means THIS is not enough. Which means I need to look for more.

Ultimately, it comes down to this. What do you want? What do YOU want? This is THE hardest question for women to answer. We create layers and layers of reasons why we can't have the things we want. We pretend we don't want them. We pretend we want something smaller. We pretend we are fine with fine. But what is it you truly want? Not the safe thing. Not the boring thing, or the 'realistic' thing. The actual thing.

I often speak to women who tell me they want to earn 100K more than they did last year. That's great. But when I meet a woman for the first time and I ask her what her current financial goal is, the first number she says is usually not the number. Want to know how I can tell? Spoiler alert. Energy doesn't lie. If you tell me you currently make 200K and you want to make 100K more, but you have no expression on your face or in your voice, and as you say it, you look like you're running through a laundry list or calculating your taxes, it's a tell. THAT'S NOT THE NUMBER. And we know when we've got to the number because the magic suddenly jumps out.

When I met Sofia for the first time, she was excited about where her business had got to. She had just celebrated her first 500K year, but she was totally flummoxed about how to increase her revenue any further. She was also sold on the limiting belief that to make more it has to be harder, which left her feeling stuck because she was exhausted and didn't have the capacity to work any harder. I imagine you've had this same thought process. We spoke about how she would like to add 100k-200k to her annual top line revenue. Her face showed nothing. She seemed like she was feeling tired. *"That's not the number,"* I said. *"So what is?"* She thought for a moment. *"Well..."* There was a long pause. I could practically FEEL the conflicting voices she was battling with. *"Can I suggest something?"* I asked. She nodded. *"From what you've told me, I don't think 600K is the number. I think it's 1 million dollars."* I like to throw this in when I speak to clients because it always gets a reaction. *"Actually, it's 1.5 million dollars"* she said and burst out laughing. She had been completely still for our conversation, but she suddenly lit up, leaning forward in her chair and her eyes shone. *"That's such a relief to say out loud!"*

And that's how we know we've found the resonant financial goal. It's such a relief to stop pretending that you're fine with fine. It's such a relief to acknowledge that you are looking for more. Imagine the progress you can make when you're not fighting yourself at every stage. When you're not sabotaging your success and fighting to make it smaller and to make yourself less, so you won't feel like you're too much. Maybe your 'more' isn't a money goal in your business—maybe it's a business activity, like a conference or a retreat. Maybe it's working at a high level that feels so high you're not even sure if you're crazy to name it. Maybe it's not something business related but there's a trip you are ready to take or a book you are ready to write or something completely different.

It could be that you have a small voice inside of you saying *"I want to go but I'm scared."* That's ok. Do it scared. You are allowed to go. You are allowed to want more. And the fun is really only getting started.

In our next two chapters we are going to look at why our too-much-ness matters at the micro level—our trauma, how this blocks us in business, and how we can hold it instead—AND at the macro level—why the world needs women like us to be bold, and more than that, become wealthy.

CHAPTER SUMMARY:

- Stop Looking Outward, Learn to Look Inward
- The Breadcrumb Trail Leading to Your 'More'
- Radical Self Improvement and Its Magical Cousin
- The Great Exchange—Switching External Validation for Internal Validation
- Starting to Envision Your 'More'
- Writing Your Permission Slip

4 Am I Broken?

So far, we have looked at what it really means to be too much, and what it means to start looking for your 'more.' But in this chapter, we are going to address an important topic that is a common experience for those of us who are too much. And that is trauma—and its impact on your business journey. This chapter is for you if you speak the language of trauma and trauma recovery.

Now you might be wondering, what is a business coach like me doing talking about trauma? What is the link between trauma and business anyway? I have to tell you, I meet women all the time who are total rockstars on the outside, but they are bleeding from emotional wounds on the inside. There is a high prevalence of trauma among women entrepreneurs, and it can sometimes start to get loud when we do business growth work. But there's an important distinction I want to make here before we jump in.

I am a brilliant coach and my work is trauma-informed, but I am not a trauma therapist. Coaching is focused around moving forward, even if it means acknowledging trauma in order to do so. We might acknowledge the existence of trauma in coaching work, but we don't delve into the trauma itself. Therapy is the place that you can do the detailed work on your trauma, and I always advise my clients to consider engaging a therapist if they haven't already. If you need help working through trauma, get the help of a trained professional. You can look one up through your insurance provider or follow the recommendation of someone you trust. Do your homework and check they have the necessary qualifications and experience, but if what I've said so far is chiming with you, and you don't want to carry it alone anymore, it helps so much to get help. Trauma *can* be healed and its impact greatly reduced with the right treatment and support.

If the subject of trauma feels triggering, remember you can skip forward to the next chapter or put the book down entirely and get yourself regulated. I want to give some reassurance here that I will do my best to not 'kick up' the substance of your trauma in the pages that follow, and also to reiterate that my goal is always to keep things feeling safe for you as my reader. But consider this your permission slip to make your own call on what feels like the right course of action for you in this moment. You can always come back when you are feeling better regulated, or maybe this just isn't the moment for this particular conversation.

Trauma and Too-Much-Ness

For some of us, our trauma is inextricably linked to our too-muchness. Are we traumatized because we are too much, or are we too much because we are traumatized? I believe in a lot of cases, it's both. Both are self-perpetuating. Similar to when we feel like we are too much, trauma can isolate us from others. With both trauma and feeling like too much, it often feels easier to mask our true self, or dumb ourselves down so we stand a chance of fitting in. And there can be a profound sense of frustration with ourselves—*"Why am I like this? Why can't I just be normal/like other people?"*—or even with the world as a whole. *"Why is it so hard for people to accept me?"* It can feel like there is something fundamentally wrong with you, and like it is the easiest thing for other people to effortlessly swim with the tide and yet we just can't seem to make it work. It's why a lot of us have ended up as entrepreneurs.

So it's not surprising that a common fear of women consultants who feel like too much is, *"Am I too messed up to succeed in my business?"* Because there is nothing like trauma to make us feel broken. Often women who are too much have experienced repeated rejection personally and professionally. Like me, you may have had an early or unwanted exit from your corporate career because of either trauma or being too much, or both, which is a traumatic experience all by itself. But you may already know that some really traumatic things have happened to you and be all too aware of the impact it has had on you. And because women are often made to feel like we are to blame for the bad things that happen to us, it is understandable to be at a place where after several decades of achievement with unhealthy side orders of frustration, rejection and disappointment, we can't help but wonder, *"Can I really do this? Can I build a seven figure business despite everything that has happened to me? Am I broken?"*

So, in this chapter, we're going to look at what trauma is and how we can better understand it, then we're going to look at what a seven figure business is and how we can better understand that, and then, how we can hold both of these things in the same space without getting triggered or thrown off course. Like everything I teach and work on with my clients, it's my goal that this will feel completely safe. In fact, when I told one of my dear clients that I was writing this book, she actually got a little tearful and said, *"Jessica, you have to write this book because people are bleeding, and you know how to make it stop."* So, this chapter is for you if you know exactly what it feels like to be bleeding from trauma that, maybe, you have got so used to experiencing that you don't even realize any more that you are in emotional pain every day.

What is Trauma?

Now it may be the case that this is not a new topic for you, but before we dive in, I want to define our terms. It could be that you have been doing the work on your trauma for decades—this is true for a lot of my clients—and you understand where it came from, and what triggers it, and you've already seen progress on your journey. It could be that your 'too-much-ness' is 100% a result of the emotional pain you have been in for years and years, but you've never connected it with trauma. So how do we understand trauma and how can you know if it applies to you?

Trauma is commonly defined as being the separation between how we experience events that are happening, in relation to previous events that *have* happened. We are affected not only by the traumatic event that happens, but also by the imprint it leaves in the body. Not only this, we often have zero or very little awareness of our trauma because it is imprinted in the subconscious mind but invisible on our bodies or in our conscious mind. Then one day it gets triggered either because we reach a crisis point, or even through surprisingly big emotional reactions we have to seemingly small things. Trauma can show up as us, in basic terms, reacting to things that are *not still happening*, only your body experiences it as if the trauma is repeating itself in the present moment. When we talk about 'triggers', this is what is being referred to—the body is reacting to something which is not happening. But it *did* happen previously—and you may or may not be conscious of the trauma that has been triggered, OR the events that originally caused it.[14]

Trauma involves 'stuckness' because we have brain and body pathways that replay the event(s) and our reaction to it or them, sometimes on a loop or sometimes only when triggered. This is one of the ways that trauma affects our day-to-day experience in our bodies and the way we interact with the world around us. It is incredibly common for the traumatized women I encounter—who by the way, are high-achievers and wouldn't necessarily seem traumatized—to respond to day-to-day business interactions in a way that actually isn't anything to do with what is going on in front of them. Instead, when trauma is reactivated in the body, it is like we are there with people, but our inner experience is a replay of traumatic events that happened sometimes decades earlier. One of the ways business and trauma become connected, or rather entangled, is that we find ourselves reacting in ways that on the surface don't make sense. But when you understand the impact of trauma on your brain and body, it is like an instruction manual that suddenly illuminates a way of engaging with the world that is completely hidden from the naked eye.

You might get an angry email from a client that, on the surface, is an unreasonable demand stemming from a simple misunderstanding and can be easily resolved. But if it triggers unresolved trauma from a particular teacher you had in elementary school who humiliated you on a regular basis, or an abusive parent whose violent rage made you feel terrified, your 6-year-old self doesn't want to write a polite and calm response—she feels like hiding under the bed, throwing something or burning the house down.

Fight or flight is a familiar phrase to most of us, but you might be less familiar with *fawn or freeze*. Fawning is where we affirm our abuser and go into people-pleasing mode to make ourselves safe. Freeze is where we just shut down and cannot react, or speak, or move. I often speak to women consultants who are experiencing *fawn* or *freeze* in difficult interactions with clients, or even with team members. These dynamics can be present in corporate teams, our families, religious communities, non-religious communities—anywhere where there are human interactions and power imbalances. We often don't understand why we feel so triggered, or why as assertive high-achievers we might find ourselves speechless in the face of criticism, or retreating into deep feelings of shame or overwhelm—unless we start to look through the lens of trauma and how it shows up in business.

It is also important to understand the difference between 'Big-T Trauma' and 'Little-t trauma.' The DSM-5 (*Diagnostic and Statistical Manual of Mental Disorders*), the American Psychiatric Association's professional reference book on mental health and brain-related conditions, helps us to differentiate between the two. Big-T Trauma involves threat to a person's body or life: such as military combat; becoming a refugee; physical, sexual or domestic violence; a serious accident; really, any situation where you might experience harm or genuinely fear for your safety or your life.[15] It is worth highlighting that a huge area of Big-T Trauma exists for people of color and the LGBT community, and that often both groups also, at the same time, experience the additional trauma of systemic abuse, which is minimized or totally denied by heterosexual white folks and mainstream white Western culture.

On the other hand, Little-t trauma can feel easier to dismiss or diminish, despite the significant impact it has. Little-t trauma is caused by situations where we felt powerless and unsafe. It might be a discernible event, such as the discovery that your partner has been unfaithful or that you are being laid off from your job. But Little-t trauma may also be experienced in patterns of neglect or emotional abuse that encompass decades of your life and span thousands of 'miniature' traumatic events— not being believed, bullying, gaslighting to name but a few. The key thing is not grading types of trauma and deciding which types of trauma are more serious or less serious. The key thing is that even if you experienced Little-t trauma, without the presence of what could be considered Big-T Trauma, your body experiences it the same way. Our bodies cannot necessarily tell the difference between Big-T Trauma and Little-t trauma. Both leave us traumatized.[16]

Before we go any further, I want to stress one important point.

It is not your fault that you experienced trauma, especially if that happened at the hands of other people. I'm not even going to say *"hurt people hurt people"*. It is not your job to understand the reasons why, or make excuses for why, people in your life or in your path made the choices they did. They bear responsibility for that and you do not. Even if they don't see it that way. Even if you've never been able to tell them that you experienced their behavior as traumatic and abusive. Even if they have their own twist on events that means they paint *you* as the one at fault, or even as the one who was abusive towards them. (This is actually super common, especially when dealing with narcissistic behavior and A-grade manipulators.) It's not your job to explain it or even understand it. You are not responsible. And that is ok.

So now we've laid the foundations, let's focus on the question that many women entrepreneurs find themselves asking:

But Seriously, Am I Too Broken to Build a Seven Figure Business?

As I have already said, it is easy to question whether as trauma survivors we have any business building a seven figure business. And I'm here to tell you that it makes sense that you might feel that way, but you are absolutely more than qualified to be heading in a seven figures direction.

Here are the four things I want to say in response:

1. Let's Be Real—Life Can Suck
2. You Don't Need to be Scared of Your Big Emotions
3. You Are At Choice
4. It's All About Understanding the Rules of the Game

1. Let's Be Real—Life Can Suck

I don't want to sound like a downer, but life can suck. It is really a matter of when—not if—we experience pain and hardship. And you might be surprised to hear a business coach who specializes in mindset say this. I mean, aren't I the kind of person you'd expect to tell you find the reframe, or the silver lining?

The thing is life can be a total butt-kick at times. That makes it sound funny. But it's not funny. Life can deliver twists and events that hurt so much you can hardly breathe. For years. And I'm not even going to pretend otherwise. Sometimes I've been through seasons where thing after thing happened, and it was all I could do to stay upright. I've already shared about my burnout experience in my 20s, that knocked the wind out of me and left me feeling like I had failed everyone including myself. But I had another season in my 30s that felt like it came out of nowhere and knocked me for six.

In the space of a year, my dad was diagnosed with end-stage liver cancer and died two months later. It all happened so fast, and, actually, it all happened backwards. He seemed like he was dying, but it took time for the doctors to work out why. The cancer advanced so aggressively there was no treatment possible. At the same time, my husband got offered a job in a city 200 miles away where we knew exactly no one, and we decided to take it. During those early months I was grieving hard for my dad, and felt so lonely at times. At the same time, I fell pregnant with my second baby. My second pregnancy was full of complications. I developed gestational diabetes which meant many, many additional medical appointments, a completely different diet I had to get my head around overnight, and multiple finger prick tests every day for nine months. I then had a second traumatic birth where all the things that hadn't got episiotomied the first time tore the second time round. And at the same time as all of that, we realized that my eldest son who was three at the time was showing signs of autism.

Honestly, in those months I felt like I couldn't catch a break. I felt like I couldn't handle the thought of the future. At times, I couldn't see a way through the exhaustion of motherhood, and the dark abysses I felt like I kept plunging into. And I'm sure you know that life can be like that. Sometimes it feels like we have the ability to move mountains if we choose to, and other times it's a continual trail of grief upon grief that we just can't keep up with. Don't get me wrong—I love mindset work. It is so incredibly valuable and it has changed my life in all kinds of ways. But nothing can change the fact that we all get touched by grief and loss and all kinds of hardships. I don't believe in toxic positivity—*"That thing that happened was actually a good thing because... [insert greetings-card level platitudes here]"*. Until a few years ago, my husband was a junior pastor in a church, and alongside our own journey, we met and sat with people experiencing all kinds of pain—bereavement, miscarriage, still birth, death of a child, death of a teenage child, sickness, eating disorders, domestic violence, marital coercion and control, marital betrayal, all kinds of grief and disappointment. As a coach, I have worked with women who have been through many, many different kinds of pain and suffering. For some, it is a season they are currently in but sometimes it will be things that happened decades earlier and it is now showing up in their business. Chronic illness, family illness, loss of a parent or spouse, divorce, financial crisis. All these things can have a profound impact on us.

And yet, if you're still here to read this, you have survived everything that life has ever thrown at you. We might face all shades of grief and heartache. We might feel like getting out of bed is actually asking too much of us at times. You might be walking wounded, but

I'm here to tell you that you are not broken. And even if you feel broken—you can heal.

2. You Don't Need to be Scared of Your Big Emotions

One of the reasons we try to avoid our trauma or, as we saw in the last chapter, we become dissociated from our bodies as a result of the painful things we have experienced, is because we are scared of our big emotions.

It feels like successful people don't have any problems. Every day we are bombarded with high-res images of people we admire looking happy, confident and like they are in total control of their lives. They are building and exiting successful businesses, hobnobbing with their thousands of high-powered friends, and talking about their amazing seven figure lifestyle. We know that the news and social media only shows us the carefully curated moments, but we still have a hard time not believing that what we are seeing isn't the whole truth. It feels like our own lives pale in comparison. But here's something you might not have ever considered. You are allowed to be in grief. You are allowed to feel angry. You are allowed to feel broken. You are allowed to question if it will ever get better. You are allowed to quit your business. You are allowed to pretend you are going to quit your business.

The key thing I want to impart here is that you don't have to be scared of your emotions. Big emotions don't mean you are broken. Big emotions don't mean you can't take over the world. You don't have to read anything more into your emotions than they are there. It is like a storm that hits, but it does also pass. Especially when you have the support of a qualified therapist.

3. You Are At Choice

And here's something else you might not have considered. I'm going to be straight with you—this might be a hard thing to hear, and I don't mean it in a dismissive or flippant way. When we feel broken, we feel disempowered. It feels like we are the victim of our circumstances or the actions of other people. When we have been betrayed or hurt by others, it is all too easy to live in constant fear of them doing something else to us or worsening the pain they have already caused.

But the thing is—you are always at choice.

Holding onto the hurt is a choice.

Letting go of the hurt is a choice.

It is ok if that doesn't feel accessible at the moment. This is a door I want to show you exists, even if you can't see it or go through it just yet. It's like the path in the forest that hasn't become clear. You might be in constant pain from your trauma, experiencing regular triggers and feeling like, *"DON'T YOU THINK IF I COULD CHOOSE SOMETHING DIFFERENT TO THIS, I WOULD HAVE DONE BY NOW?"* You know, with the urge to slam some doors, or throw something at me?

When big reactions happen, it can often mean your Inner Child has been activated—we'll dig more into this in Part 2 of this book. But one of the most powerful moments for me, in my journey of processing my lifelong trauma, was a comment that a business friend made during a peer mastermind retreat. She said to me, *"Jessica, I want you to know that at the moment you are choosing to inhabit your trauma 100%. And that is always an option that's open to you. But you can also put it down and decide not to carry it with you any more. You can choose that at any time."*

And the weird thing is, I could have received that as an insult. I could have taken it as something that minimized my pain and trivialized everything I had been battling to hold for years. I was experiencing daily migraines. My anxiety was so high it felt like at times I couldn't breathe. My trauma meant I felt profoundly unsafe in my day-to-day life even though I was several decades on from the events I was reacting to, and my business was growing fast—which only made me feel even more unsafe. But I received my friend's words—that I could choose to put my trauma down at any time—as a beautiful gift. It didn't happen overnight, but I realized I could cut the threads that tied me to this trauma, one strand at a time, and I could become a separate entity.

It took time, a lot of therapy, a lot of EMDR. My trauma recovery work isn't done, but it is easier to hold than it used to be. And the gift I received in that moment was the profound realization that we are always at choice. It's not easy to choose to let it go. For the longest time, I couldn't let go of my trauma. It all felt so unresolved. How do you move on when the people who have left you with so much hurt don't even think they did anything, let alone acknowledge and apologize? How can you move on, when they seem like they are living their best life and flourishing in every possible way?

They say that unforgiveness is the poison we drink hoping that the other party will die. I'm not going to tell you to forgive your past trauma if you're not ready to. I don't know that we have to forgive people who aren't seeking our forgiveness. But at the same time, forgiveness is choosing to free ourselves. And the gift I want to give you is the knowledge that we are always at choice. We can always choose, and this is such an important part of the journey of looking for your 'more.'

Some people stay in trauma their whole lives, and honestly, I don't blame them one bit. Sometimes it feels impossible to even get out of bed. And, as you already know, after my burnout episode I barely got out of bed for seven months. It's impossible to look at the horizon and see anything other than the pain we are in, and the injustice of it all.

But we can always choose something better. Even if it is just 1% better, or 0.01% better, each time. And if this feels hard to hear at the moment—that is ok. You are allowed to be kind of mad with me for making it sound simple and easy when we both know it is anything but. But please know, I am not saying this from a place of, *"I have never struggled"* or, *"I have overcome everything hard that has ever happened to me"*. Sometimes I feel like I have built a beautiful life and everything hard is behind me. Sometimes I feel like I am right back in it and still bleeding. We are always at choice.

A coach of mine used to say, *"If you say so."* It was SO ANNOYING but at the same time so helpful. Our words are powerful. We forget this. We think no one is listening and we have no power to influence anything but if there's one thing I've learned it's this: people are always listening. But more than that—WE are always listening to ourselves. Have you heard the saying that *"worry is praying for the things you DON'T want to happen"?* The things we focus our minds around matter, whether we're thinking in positive or negative terms. If you've had a coach before, you might notice that sometimes it feels like a game of 'word correction.' You know that dynamic where everything you say, your coach gives you the side eye and is like, *Nope. Reframe that thought, please.* Again, it's super annoying but it is IMPORTANT because we believe 100% of the words we say to ourselves.

Whenever we take bold action in life or in business it follows this pattern:

Think the belief.
Say the belief.
Act out the belief.
Receive the belief.

This is 100% true whether we are thinking empowering thoughts that build us up or disempowering thoughts that cut us down. YOU are listening to the words you say. Are you broken? Or are you walking wounded? Healing? Surviving? Thriving? You get to choose.

If you say so.

And on that note:

4. It's All About Understanding the Rules of the Game

If we have the gift of choice, then it follows logically that we might choose to label ourselves as 'broken', but we can just as easily choose the label of 'not broken.' It is ok to feel broken sometimes, and just as ok not to choose to see ourselves that way. But we need to understand the rules of the game when it comes to building a successful seven figure business. I genuinely believe that most men know this instinctively, but women need to hear this many times before we can believe it:

- *You don't need to be perfect to have an amazing business*
- *You can be walking wounded AND still make a ton of money*
- *You can be a hot mess AND still make a ton of money*
- *Money and success are not a reward for doing everything flawlessly*

It's like apples and oranges. You and your business are linked but not the same. Stop believing that you have to be the good girl, or get the A-grade, because this is not how you play the game of business. It's not about you and how well you're doing at life. It's about the market value of the services you provide and how effectively you get them in front of the right clients and deliver. It is that simple.

Let's be real—you can make a ton of money without delivering at your highest level. You can make a ton of money delivering something that is poor quality. I bet you can think of dozens of examples, without even trying, of products and services that were in high demand and had high ticket pricing that did not deliver the goods or value for money. And the companies offering them got rich just the same.

It may not be an aligned way to do business but the money is paid because the client believes that you can deliver what you say you can. And, for the record, this is why it's so incredibly annoying when other people make a ton more money than you when you know they're not delivering the high standard of service you know you would.

You need to hear this—stop playing the wrong game.

You can be a hot mess and still have a fantastic business. You can be a work in progress and make the money you want to make. You can make even more money than that and not be the finished article. You don't need to be perfect, or insta-famous, or have a flawless appearance, or a million celebrity friends. All you need is to be good enough. And we already know you are 1000% good enough. Even with your trauma. Even with your too-much-ness. Actually, as you know by now, your too-much-ness is all part of the magic that makes you stand out from the crowd. How awesome is that?!

I know it can feel like we need to be superhuman in order to be worthy of business success. But I have to tell you—I have been able to build a lucrative business that I love even though there are all kinds of things about me that have often felt to me like barriers to success. There are no catches, no smoke and mirrors. I do 100% of my own coaching. I am the breadwinner for my family. My business revenue has completely transformed my lifestyle (and my tax bracket!). I work 3-4 hours per day, 3-4 days per week. I take at least 13 weeks holiday a year when my kids have school holidays. I travel internationally to host retreats for my clients in exotic locations. And my favorite part? I drink my coffee from a mug that says, "*I do a thing called what I want.*" Yes, I do.

But this has all been something I've built after my corporate career ended when I was only 27, and I was left with the ashes of a life I thought would look totally different. I experienced Complex PTSD for several years, and I am still doing trauma recovery work. I've actually wondered for a lot of years if I have autism and ADHD—my brain just doesn't work like a neurotypical brain and my anxiety is often high. I have experienced chronic illness and have been severely energy limited for a lot of my adult life. None of these things have stopped me from achieving the success I want. The only thing that came close to stopping me was *me*—and my fear that all my personal mess meant I couldn't be successful at business.

All of the things I've said about my success are true. So are all of the shortcomings I've shared above. They can both be true at the same time. I have a total inability to present myself as if I've always been confident and I have a perfect life. No one has a life without mess or pain. Everyone gets burned sometimes.

Dear Reader, I know you have gone through some things. I know that sometimes it feels like you are never going to see the light of day with all of the pain and the trauma and the work you have to do. I can promise you—you don't have to have it all figured out in order to make a success of your business, to find the most amazing life fulfillment, and make a ton of money getting paid to do the work you are so awesome at it doesn't even feel like work.

In summary, are you broken? This is something you have to decide. This is something you GET to decide. You are at choice. *Are* you broken? It's another *if you say so* moment.

I am aware that this chapter might feel like it has been a lot. I shed some tears writing it, not because I'm sad but because I feel this with my whole body. If you are in a situation where you have never had anyone acknowledge your trauma or apologize to you when they really fucking should have apologized, and this makes you feel like it is probably your fault, or not a big deal—my heart goes out to you. And I am here to speak to this.

If you don't feel the need to minimize your trauma any more but that in itself feels like the hardest pill to swallow—know that you are not alone. Sometimes, it is easier in the short term to deny it all or make it smaller. It is easier to feel like the problem probably was us, because the alternative—that we *aren't* wrong, and we *have* been disregarded and mistreated—breaks your heart a thousand times over. My heart goes out to you too—and I am here to speak to this.

All we can do is do the work. Process the trauma and allow the body to heal. It isn't always quick, but it isn't something you have to carry forever. It can be healed. I have experienced this. I have clients who are experiencing this. Trauma doesn't have to stop you from achieving everything you want to achieve and more.

And if you've made it this far through this chapter—this is an awesome achievement. I am cheering for you! If you need to put this book down and care for yourself—go right ahead. The next chapter will be ready and waiting when you're ready to jump back in.

Now we've looked at what it means to be too much and looking for more in the 'micro' aspect—for you as a person in overcoming your trauma and your fear that you may be broken—let's also look at what this means in the 'macro' sense, because looking for your 'more' is fully about you, the person, but also fully about the entire world, and every woman on the planet.

Pretty cool, hey?

I can't wait to see you there!

CHAPTER SUMMARY:

- Trauma and Too-Much-Ness
- What is Trauma?
- But Seriously, Am I Too Broken to Build a Seven Figure Business?
- 1. Let's Be Real—Life Can Suck
- 2. You Don't Need to be Scared of Your Big Emotions
- 3. You Are At Choice
- 4. It's All About Understanding the Rules of the Game

5 The World Needs More Wealthy Women

In Chapter 4, we zoomed in to how our too-much-ness can intersect with trauma in our backstory to create a perfect storm of stuckness in our consulting businesses. When we better understand that being too much is a good thing, and that with the right support we can do the work of healing our trauma and setting it down—even when this is a work in progress—it frees us up to achieve the business success we want. That way, we don't have to bring it all with us on the journey which, as you probably know, slows us all the way down.

In this chapter, I want us to zoom out together and look at the bigger picture. It matters that we learn to hold our too-much-ness correctly, so you are free to fulfill your potential and create wealth through your consulting business. And this matters not just for you or me, but for women all over the world, past, present and future.

The 'W Word'

Did you notice that I used the 'W word' just then? That's right.

Wealth.

It is so important that, as women, we make our peace with both the concept and the reality of wealth. Receiving it. Holding it. Stewarding it. Investing it. Maybe even wielding it. And one day, passing it on to the next generation.

I meet women all the time who are really uncomfortable with this word, although there is one more word that tends to bring another strong reaction:

RICH.

Women say to me all the time, *"I don't want to be seen as someone who is rich."* And this makes me smile a little, because, honestly, my kids love the concept of being rich. It seems like quite a few of the playground conversations that happen during the school day revolve around whose parents are rich. Apparently, some are billionaires. (I happen to know with complete certainty that this is not the case, living in an ex-industrial city in the North of England, but I love that these are the things some kids are boasting about!) But the very fact that as children we dream of being rich and feel completely at ease with the concept, and yet as adult women it seems like something has come in and stolen that from us. And I have some theories about what that likely is.

The Fear of Money

It is always fascinating when I do money mindset work with clients that there is a near-universal fear among women that they will become a depraved version of themselves if they increase their wealth. And there can be a common misperception here, too, that the Bible itself says that *"money is the root of all evil"*, but as someone who was a pastor's wife for 12 years, let me just clarify that the verse actually says that "the *love of money* is a root of all kinds of evil."[17] (My italics)

Money itself is neutral. We have often been raised to view money as corrupting, something that brings out the worst in people, and while this can be true (just google the word 'inheritance' and at least 10 million incredibly depressing examples will immediately flood your screen)—my view is that money is a useful tool for making some things in life easier.

We can use money to make our lives easier and more comfortable, and we can also use money to help others. I don't know about you, but I have done life with almost no money, and I am now able to do life with more and—sorry not sorry—I would choose life with money every time. It is just better. But have you noticed some 'all or nothing thinking' creeping in again here? Because our choice isn't just '*be rich and a bad person*' or '*be poor but a nice person*'. There are a thousand options in between. It's way more nuanced than that—and we need to break the association of how much money we have with the kind of person we are. We also need to stop acting like this is something we have no control over. Making more money doesn't have to mean that you will lose sight of your values—of course, it could happen if you choose to abandon your ideals, but you could just as easily make the money you desire AND retain the values you hold right now. It is really just a story we choose to tell ourselves, and more often than not, it keeps us stuck in scarcity.

Recovering from Money Trauma

It is really tempting to hold onto our money scarcity even when we are not experiencing money scarcity. I see this all the time with clients who have drastically increased their personal net worth. Money trauma is a literal real thing—and, just like any other brain pathway, we will stay with the one we are used to even when our material circumstances change. And we will find it hard, at first, to allow a new pathway to form.

When my husband and I first got married, he was training at a Christian seminary to be a pastor and it was great for around six months because my job in London meant I could support us both. But after my burnout episode, during my seven-months-in-bed phase, I opted for voluntary redundancy and unsurprisingly, this meant our money security basically evaporated overnight. We were looking at our finances for that year and we didn't have enough money coming in to pay our rent, let alone eat. And even though that too-exhausted-to-get-out-of-bed phase did end, leading to me getting back into work and within a couple of years running and growing a start-up consultancy firm that would lead to me eventually setting up on my own as a business coach, I was all too aware that for several years after we were out of the money crisis, I would experience rising panic every time I looked at our household finances spreadsheet. My heart would start to pound, and I would feel all hot and clammy. Sometimes, I had to calculate and recalculate everything multiple times because although I could see everything was in the black, my body was convinced I had made a mistake, and we were back in the red.

And I speak to women all the time who experience this, too. We can feel this sense of panic whether we have $100 in the bank or $100,000. And it is always super interesting that the women who have the biggest financial reserves in their business and in their personal finances can experience *more* money anxiety than women who have all kinds of credit card debt and no reserves at all.

Here's something I have noticed when it comes to women and money.

We think the money itself will provide security and fulfillment, but actually what we want is the FEELING of security and fulfillment.

And the hard truth that almost no one wants to hear? We crave the external validation of money in the bank, but the thing that gives us the most peace is the INTERNAL validation that can only come from us choosing to step into Radical Self Acceptance.

We have already talked about internal validation vs external validation, and I want to mark it for your attention here as well, because it's a neat little concept that can change EVERYTHING in our lives and businesses. Whenever we look for external things as validation, we end up giving away our power to those things. When we prioritize internal validation, we create the emotional state we need to achieve the external validation.

And yet, if given the choice, we will nearly always go first for the external thing. *Give me the money now, please, and THEN I will feel good about myself.* It sounds convincing, even plausible doesn't it? But when you give yourself the internal validation first through Radical Self Acceptance, you're creating energy that attracts money. And the good news is that this is a transformation you are in complete control of—we can influence our internal state so much more than we can control the externals of money and success, let alone the economy or national/world politics. You can't control for example whether your prospective client will sign their contract with you within the next 24 hours, but you *can* do the work to feel calm and find a perspective on it that feels like it serves you. This is why it's such a powerful journey to learn how to hold our too-much-ness and feel for our 'more'—because the very act of finding the life and business that make your too much feel like just the right amount is all about you creating a stable inner life FIRST and then receiving the external validation of that, second.

This can feel so unfair and sometimes it even feels like we are doing something wrong if the money is taking time to show up. But rather than quit and abandon your business, this is the time to lean in like you never have before.

It's About Money, but It's About More than Just Money

We need bold women who understand that it's about money, but it's also about way more than just the money. As we've seen, money by itself is neutral. But it enables us to live differently—both in terms of lifestyle and the emotions we feel. The life I get to lead because of my business isn't just about the material things. Wealth means protection from many of the hardships of life and it can also mean we can live in ways that some might consider luxurious. It means we can create agency and create meaningful change not just for ourselves, but also for the women around us and the future generations of women to come. But there is also the emotional benefit of the healing work we are required to do in order to flourish in business. I used to do the healing work because it enabled me to do my business. These days, it's the other way around—I do my business because it enables me to do the healing work that is transforming the way I show up in my life and my business. Money has enabled me to do this work but the positive benefits are priceless. And you can experience this too.

It's great to have money but the long-term benefit of doing the healing work is not just that we get bigger businesses and more money. It's that we experience healing, and we are freed from the trauma cycles that have been playing out in our bodies and brains for decades. And often, these trauma cycles have been playing out for generations. And they will keep doing so until someone in the family is able to face it head on and break the cycle.[18] This is why it is about money, but it is also about more than money. You cannot put a price on experiencing freedom from trauma. Feeling like you are enough, and you are safe, is life-changing—for you, which is the most wonderful news, but the impact of this healing work will be felt by everyone in your world and the generations that follow. Learning self love, learning Radical Self Acceptance, is life-changing. It positively impacts your relationships, your business, your inner life, your health and wellbeing. It affects every part of everything in your world.

It's about money but it's also about more than money.

It's About Correcting the Inequities of the Past

The key reason that we need to pursue a positive relationship with money and the concept of wealth is that for women, wealth = agency. In a world where women are so routinely disregarded and overlooked, where for centuries women were barred from holding property and were treated as possessions, this matters.

As an undergrad student I was able to study the Transatlantic Slave Trade between Europe, Africa and North America as part of my History degree, and to this day I am so glad that my university invested in teaching such a forward-thinking area of academic study. We were taught about the realities of slavery and the slave trade that so many people have no idea about even today. Before the nineteenth century in America, enslaved colored women (and men) were legally considered to be property and literal possessions of their white owners.[19] In academic discourse, we talk about intersections of race and gender, because the legacy still persists today with Hispanic women earning 65 cents on the dollar, women of color 70 cents and white women 82 cents.[20] In addition, just 2% of investment funding goes to woman-owned businesses in the USA[21] and just 10% of Fortune 500 and FTSE 100 companies are led by female CEOs[22]. I think we can all agree that if there is one thing that would change the lives of women the world over, it is greater agency.

So what do I mean by agency? I mean the sense of control and the ability to make decisions about our own lives—the ability to be an 'agent' in your own life, to have equal access to education and career opportunities. Access to finance and investment in business. So many women entrepreneurs have boot-strapped and self-funded our businesses, to the point that we see it as normal. We often can't invest in the support and professional services we need to grow our businesses because we simply don't have the cash. Men do not approach business in this way—accessing capital and credit that women are routinely denied or are not even educated about.

To have agency would mean no longer being excluded from back rooms and the places where '*men do business*'. There are so many rooms that as women, we cannot get into, and so many tables where we can't get a seat. It is estimated that it will take 200 years to close the gender pay gap in the corporate world.[23] Because let's be honest, they don't really want to do that. But as women entrepreneurs, we can close that gap in an instant. Put your prices up. Charge for your consulting services with the confidence that would be yours if you were a straight, white male. You could even do it today. I am obsessed with entrepreneurship because it creates a viable path for women to access these decision-making spaces that we have been barred from, but more than that, to create our own ecosystem of rooms and tables.

And yet, it makes perfect sense why our generation of women in the West still carry trauma around money and feel imposter syndrome due to lingering structural exclusion, because we are among the first women in history to have so much opportunity. Even going back two generations in my own family—neither of my grandmothers went to university. Neither of them could drive. One was an unpaid carer for the elderly relatives in her family alongside being a wife and mother, and the other was widowed in her 30s and worked as a church cleaner and school dinner lady until she was 80. My mother's generation of baby boomers were the first to normalize college education for women, but the lack of availability of childcare and—let's be honest—rampant sexism and misogyny in the 1970s and 1980s, meant many women had to take huge career gaps to raise children that left a permanent impact on their career aspirations, access to career opportunities and status in society generally.

Now we get to be part of a generation of women who have never had so much opportunity—and yet we are still so far from equality with the lives that would have been our birthright if we were born male. As a woman who chose to have children (and feels lucky to have been able to do so), I remember the moment I realized that my career path was a truncated path with stops and starts for pregnancy, child birth and child rearing, whereas my husband's was a straight run from college to retirement. I remember thinking, *wow the things I would be able to do professionally if I had a path as straight as that!*

So then, if entrepreneurship creates the opportunity for us to level the playing field and overcome the setbacks and hand we were dealt, why does it feel so overwhelming to be able to create extravagant wealth as entrepreneurs and consultants? I believe that for most of us, we have had a scarcity of role models from the generations of women who have come before us. And this is no criticism of those women. In economic terms and, frankly, in quite a few other ways, they got dealt a raw hand. The women who came before us often didn't get to live out their dreams. They were discouraged from having them because it was so unlikely they would be able to pursue them. But we do. It's an amazing privilege—but that doesn't make it easy to know how to hold it all. And it also doesn't mean that we *aren't* swimming against the tide in order to get there. Even though you crack a door to a room of decision-makers, it doesn't mean you are welcome once you are there, or that you didn't have to bust your ass to get to the table.

But all of this is why it is so great to be too much! You don't need to live a small, frustrated life where you have to sacrifice your fulfillment for the sake of domestic equanimity. Your too-much-ness is the driving force that propels you out of the life that doesn't fit, and into the life that does.

Fulfillment Is Good, Peak Fulfillment Is Better

It's a major life-hack, as we saw in Chapter 2, to have the realization that high fulfillment exists, and is a key ingredient to making your too-much-ness feel like just the right amount. But there is actually an option that lies beyond high fulfillment because you also have the opportunity to step into your 'Peak Fulfillment'—your life's highest point where you are achieving the fullest version of the things you have the capability to. And this can be anything from a successful consulting business, a glittering speaking career, building a legacy family home to enjoy with your children and grandchildren, developing creative talents, mentoring others. It's not so much having a bucket list, as having experiences where you feel like it finally makes sense why you have appeared in the world and been able to share your gifts with others.

I do the bulk of my work with women in their mid to late 40s and 50s, and I see women all the time who are aligning their career experience and subject matter expertise in ways that deliver glimpses of this peak fulfillment. I love seeing them shine because of their gifts and experience, but also because of the amazing confidence that comes from being a woman in your prime and not having to play the game of pleasing others any more. It's not just a vanity exercise or one woman creating her own privilege. As women, we all have a vital role to play in changing the story for all women everywhere and future generations of women. In changing your story, you are changing *their* story. Becoming the role model you didn't have. Opening doors and keeping them open for the next generation. Building your own rooms and your own damn table.

I would love to think that somewhere in the world there is a small-statured woman like me who has felt excluded from the corporate workplace similarly to me, who can look at what I am doing and know that she can also forge her own path and create fabulous amounts of money. I know that there are women out there who need to see *your* journey to know they can set out on theirs. And for us, as women consultants, this matters.

Any woman who generates more than $100,000 in annual revenue as an entrepreneur is in the top 10% of all women entrepreneurs out there. Estimates suggest that just 2% of women entrepreneurs get to seven figures.[24] We need more women breaking the glass ceiling of six figure and seven figure revenue so we can create more access for other women, more role models, and more paths forged. And the research shows that far from women pushing men out of the way, when women thrive, the men in their lives do too in the form of greater prosperity and closer family ties through being freed up to be more involved in their kids' lives.[25] The Alison Rose Report on female entrepreneurship in the UK stated that £250 billion could be added to the UK economy if women entrepreneurs received greater funding and support.[26] And I imagine the number is significantly higher for women entrepreneurs in the USA. Women don't just take up space—we boost our national economies! And we need to normalize what it looks like for women to create wealth. Studies show that one of the most significant predictors of economic wellbeing for our children, and the generations that follow, is to be able to pass down generational wealth.[27] This is something that women entrepreneurs create the ability to do—in spades.

But you might be reading this and thinking, *"ugh, Jessica I don't want to have to become an online influencer with a huge seven figure empire of low-quality courses and exhausting, sprawling membership communities"*. And this is the amazing thing, because as a consultant you don't need to follow the B2C (business to consumer) blueprint of how to scale a business in that way. Consulting businesses generally follow a B2B (business to business) model which can be far simpler and more streamlined. As a business coach who has career experience in the public and private sectors, with four years experience growing a start-up and 10 years building my own business working with hundreds of women entrepreneurs, I have to tell you—there is not just *one way* to structure and grow your business.

And one of the reasons I love to work with women consultants is because when it comes to women entrepreneurs, you, ladies, are the elite.

One of the guidelines I set for my clients is this—*from now on, your minimum contract size is $100,000.* It's not a hard and fast rule. Some of my clients are working with a $50,000 or $80,000 core contract blueprint. But the reason we shoot for this is that, firstly, as a subject matter expert, you are able to work at a high level. In fact, several of my clients routinely sell contracts at $200,000-$400,000. But secondly, when you make high ticket sales to corporate organizations who are looking for your consulting experience and subject matter expertise in this way, it means that you need far fewer sales in order to get to $1 million. If you are selling a $100,000 consulting offer, that is just 10 sales to get to seven figures. And by the way, if you get only one of those $100,000 contracts, you just brought in more revenue than 90% of women entrepreneurs out there. If you can make it a $250,000 consulting offer, that could be just four clients. With no need for a bulky sales force or huge delivery team. And the thing I often say is, if you're going to make three to four sales this year, wouldn't you rather make $750,000-$1,000,000 than $15,000-$20,000?

You Are Exceptional

One of the things I have noticed time and again in my work with women entrepreneurs is that we are incredibly good at so many things, but we fail woefully in one specific area. We do not understand how exceptional, how gifted, how talented, we actually are. How high the standard of our work is. How well other people think of us. How much we are worth every cent of the big money we are paid.

Instead, as we saw in Chapter 1, we so often go through life believing we are average, or even that we are deficient in some way. We assume that everyone can do what we can do. We're not special, which means our skills are not exceptional. And just like me with my promotion when I was 19, we are flabbergasted when we receive the recognition we have earned. Note: the recognition WE HAVE EARNED. We may tell ourselves and others that we don't understand why we got the praise and recognition, the pay rise, the new job, the award, but we are often the only ones who can't see it.

One of the things I've noticed when I speak to women entrepreneurs, and more broadly, women in general, is that we so often assume that what we are good at isn't particularly impressive, and actually, probably everyone can do it. We are so ready to cast ourselves as generic, we don't understand how exceptional we truly are. We can get stuck in a thought loop between the belief that we are incredibly special and lacking recognition, and the countering belief that we are truly nothing special. While you are in a season where your business doesn't yet reflect your true potential, it can be a really hard tension to hold. And this is even more so the case for those of us with trauma in our backstory. Our trauma magnifies our failings. We may have been told we are to blame for the traumatic experiences we received. So, we internalize, and instead of seeing how bright and shiny we are, we get it all wrong and assume the worst. And for neurodivergent women, our Inner Critic is often magnified and on red alert.

Too often, we see the world in terms of the journey from 'good to great' or 'average to exceptional', not realizing that most people are still struggling to get to good. And they don't even lose any sleep about it.

So, let's get clear on some facts for a moment. You are exceptional, whether you're a woman entrepreneur, a woman consultant, a woman leader. If you are made to feel like you're too much, this is actually a sign that you set the bar WAY higher than most people. And the result of this is you drive yourself hard to achieve Radical Self Improvement, and, as a by-product, you achieve excellence in most of the things you do.

I bet, as you read this, you are making a list of the things you don't feel you are good at. *But I gained those 10lb. And my house is a mess.* (Is it though? LOL) *And I hate my hair. And I should be so much further forward than I am.* Remember, if you have a six figure or more business, you are in the top 10% of women entrepreneurs. If you have a seven figure business, that puts you in the top 2% of women entrepreneurs. Even if you don't yet have a six figure business but you have the drive and potential to do it in the future.

You are exceptional, my friend. You are NOT average or 'the norm'.

And my question for you is, what would your world look like, and feel like, if you started to powerfully bring yourself and your perception of yourself into proper alignment? If you could see yourself the way the rest of us do?

I'm guessing you would be, and feel, unstoppable.

The world needs more wealthy women. The world needs more women who know they are made for more, and the evidence that this is true for you is that you feel like too much.

So now that I've made the case for why too much matters for us as individuals but also for us in terms of the whole world, let's look at the practicalities of how we actually go on this journey of looking for more.

CHAPTER SUMMARY:

- The 'W Word'
- The Fear of Money
- Recovering from Money Trauma
- It's About Money, but It's About More than Just Money
- It's About Correcting the Inequities of the Past
- Fulfillment Is Good, Peak Fulfillment Is Better
- You Are Exceptional

PART TWO

How To Look for Your 'More'— In Pursuit of Peak Fulfillment

In Part One, we looked at what it truly means to be too much. We explored that as someone who feels like too much, you need to look for your 'more', and why, when you have trauma in your backstory, this is hard. But 'hard' isn't what stops you. So often, the boulder in your path is not knowing what you have to do next in order to look for—and find—your 'more'.

Remember our mantra:

> ***When I feel like too much. It means THIS is not enough. Which means I need to look for more.***

I'm sure you're wondering, *this all sounds great, Jessica, but what does it mean to start this kind of journey and how do I even do that?*

Or you might be asking, *what if I don't know what 'more' looks like for me?*

How do I find something I haven't given a proper shape or name to yet?

What do I do when I feel like I've found it, but it hasn't worked out the way I expected?

I wonder if you have ever had the experience of having an idea that seems so perfect and 'meant for you'. Because it feels like all the stars are aligning for you with your big idea, you assume the next step is *Execute The Big Idea.* And at first, it feels like it's working. You set out on the journey, confident that your big and bold vision will carry you where you need to go, and you jump in with both feet. It would be crazy not to!

You push beyond your comfort zone—after all, every online business expert says you should, right? And you are ready to go big or go home. You feel bold, brave and unstoppable. Your shields are up. You are sure you are showing up powerfully as your Next Level Self, and everything feels abundant and glorious.

Only then, out of nowhere you hit a bump in the road.

Maybe your goal doesn't happen as quickly as you expect, or the path to it doesn't work out exactly the way you anticipated that it would. For whatever reason, the project doesn't fly out of the gate. People don't seem to get it. They don't say yes, they say no.

And suddenly it's like a giant roadblock in front of you. All your abundance energy vanishes, and you find yourself rapidly cooling on the whole vision. Overwhelm kicks in hard. *What was I thinking?! I can't do this!* And you hastily pull a 180 and retreat back home, cancelling everything and feeling like you are all the way back at square one but with some extra bumps and bruises to your ego.

I call this 'mindset whiplash', and it's an important concept for us to notice at this point in the journey. Let's explore this in a little more detail because there are two ways we get it wrong when mindset whiplash kicks in.

Susannah's Story

Susannah was a top executive at a Fortune 500 firm before she started her own consulting company. She quickly built a 300K revenue consulting firm where she was the solo consultant, but she always knew she had the spark of an idea for something bigger. Over time, she realized that her 'more' was a nationwide community for high-impact ex-corporate women entrepreneurs, where they could access support, mentoring and inspiration as a group. She created a business plan and set plans in motion to launch the first group, signing up speakers and delivery partners.

Despite building a strong brand and posting consistently on social media, it was much harder to fill the group than she expected. She had seen the internet meme for entrepreneurs that says, "*If you build it, they will come*". But she built it, and... crickets. She was aiming for 12 participants in the initial cohort, but only three women signed up. Two weeks later, one of those women asked for her money back. Susannah was crushed. The group had turned out so different to what she had hoped for. She'd had a vision for herself as leader of group of women with strong voices. She'd dreamed of what this movement of women could achieve. She was embarrassed by how hard it had been to persuade women to join.

She felt like a failure.

After a few sleepless nights, Susannah decided to scrap the group and just forget the whole thing. She emailed her list of speakers to let them know she wouldn't need their services after all, and went back to her consulting business as if nothing had happened. She brushed it off and didn't offer much in the way of an explanation, but underneath she was mortified at how it had all turned out.

Lauren's Story

Or there's Lauren, who had three years of done-for-you consulting experience under her belt, since leaving her high-powered corporate job. Whatever the client asked for, she did, but she often felt like she didn't love the work, and the done-for-you approach felt dull. She knew she had the experience to work at a much higher level instead of just using 3% of her brain power, skills and experience.

Lauren's spark of an idea for something bigger was to work with the biggest brands in the industry. She rewrote her LinkedIn profile using bold and confident language to claim her ground, demonstrating she believed she was more than qualified to do this work. And she was—it made perfect sense. But a few days after taking this bold step, she felt sick with anxiety. What would people think of her, blowing her own trumpet and making out that she was the best in the industry? A phrase she saw online kept floating into her mind—*"Authority is not self-ordained"*.

She wanted to delete the whole thing and wished she had never changed it. Instead of filling her pipeline as she'd hoped, she canceled the calls she'd set up only days before. She changed her LinkedIn profile back to what it had been and she carried on with low-paid freelance consulting, feeling furious with herself and like she had embarrassed herself in front of the whole world.

Both Susannah and Lauren experienced mindset whiplash, and for them it resulted in the urge to do the 180 on the road to 'more' and flee. But here's another story that illustrates the other way we get it wrong when mindset whiplash hits.

The Room of Discouragement

Sometimes when mindset whiplash kicks in we don't flee home, but we also don't move forward in the way we did before. Where initially we felt focused and like we couldn't fail, our bump in the road experience has shaken our confidence profoundly and we don't feel as safe to run far and run fast. It is only too easy to act from fear, and we may be moving forward but we are not connected to abundance and not enjoying the journey. And I call this arriving in the *Room of Discouragement.*

I often imagine the Room of Discouragement as a dull and dreary waiting room. You know, the kind of uninspiring, clinical space with tired magazines about nothing very interesting, where you feel you might be unwittingly taking part in a psychological experiment on how long participants will wait for no actual reason. If there was a sign on the wall of this room it would say *"Abandon Hope All Ye Who Enter Here"*, because when we fall into resistance and find ourselves in the Room of Discouragement it feels like everything we just created by connecting to abundance gets turned upside down. Our motivation vanishes. We find ourselves pretending we don't actually want the things we know we clearly do want. *It's all just impossible anyway*, we mutter. We doubt our Higher Self. We scorn ourselves for having believed in abundance. It feels like waking up from a dream, and realizing what we thought we were doing in real life was all in our subconscious.

My Story

As you know, I've been in business for 10 years and in that time, frankly, I have had more failed launches than I can count—along with probably hundreds of experiences of mindset whiplash. One that particularly stands out in my memory is in the second year of my coaching business. I had a promising first year where I signed some good clients and hit my annual revenue goal, but suddenly in my second year I found myself going through a dry patch. It was that startling phenomenon of *low-hanging fruit* —and subsequently realizing I had inadvertently exhausted the local network in the town where I lived in my first year, leading to the realization that I would need to widen the net to go any further. The problem was—I had no idea how to make it happen. I was just starting to learn about the opportunities that online business could provide, but I hadn't started getting leads yet and it felt like the well had run dry. I was feeling the pressure mount up. Not only had my business ground to a halt, I had picked up some credit card debt buying courses to teach me how to get started online and was now starting to panic that I might not be able to pay it down. I made some early enquiries about quitting the business and getting a job instead, and had some positive conversations with a local recruitment agency, but they weren't able to place me anywhere. Even my efforts to abandon my failing business failed!

This was a big turning point for me. I felt the mindset whiplash big time. *Why did you sign up for those courses?! Why did you even start this business??* My Inner Critic was loud, and very happy to tell me exactly what I had done wrong. I felt huge shame over the credit card debt and like far from making more money than I could dream of, I was in danger of wrecking our finances without a plan to bring us back from that. I had a seat ready and waiting for me in the Room of Discouragement. But I didn't quit my business, even though I probably should have done at that point.

Because here's the thing about me—I am incredibly stubborn (and if you feel like too much, I imagine you probably are too—it's actually one of our superpowers!). And I looked at the situation of no clients vs no job opportunities, and realized the quickest solution to my problem was to just sign a single client. I say this to clients often, usually one client sale will make the difference between despair and solvency, so it becomes the quickest route to recovery. Just sign one client.

I didn't know it at the time, but I was overcoming mindset whiplash. Sounds great right? But I was doing it in a way that was far from aligned. I didn't flee home, but I spent more time than I should have done in the Room of Discouragement in the months that followed my bump in the road, regretting everything, feeling full of shame that it was all suddenly so hard, and questioning whether I would ever get back on the path I wanted. But I didn't just sit there. Granted—my approach was basically throwing myself repeatedly at the same brick wall, thinking that if I can just smash into it enough times, I'll crack it. And I put myself to work! My inner drill sergeant was only too happy to start calling the shots. I joined groups online, posted in Facebook groups, met women through 1:1 connection calls, and forced myself to do all the things I had been resisting. In the process, I got removed from a couple of Facebook groups (huge trigger for rejection sensitive dysphoria in case you're wondering!), heard the word 'no' an awful lot, and did all kinds of visibility, like live-streaming that I really didn't want to. And none of it felt good because the whole time I was drenched in gut-wrenching fear. It was scarcity on steroids, let alone abundance!

But even though it was done in the wrong way—full of fear and self-loathing!—it did somehow achieve the right results over time. One sale led to another as I got my online business off the ground. The credit card debt got paid off. And many years later I do now have a successful coaching business that has generated 7 figures in revenue, a popular podcast, some seriously amazing women consultants as clients, and a good reputation in my industry. I do 100% of my own coaching, I haven't done anything dark or shady to get to where I am, and as much as anything can, my business is basically what it looks like from the outside. But. I know I could have done it way sooner, and with way less grief, if I wasn't so intent on throwing myself at the same wall, time and time again, and if I hadn't been so fixed in my thinking about 'how' it had to happen.

If I had known how to engage my intuition and find the path that felt good and aligned, instead of white-knuckling a path that has often terrified me and stretched me immeasurably, I suspect it could have been a much easier ride. With far less ugly crying along the journey!

Want to know the missing ingredient and why I spent so much time that year in the Room of Discouragement?

It's because I didn't know about abundance.

As high-achieving women, we have often achieved everything we have done by dedication, self-discipline and an iron will that stops us from quitting until we get there. It's the pattern we learn in school, at university and in our corporate careers. Perseverance is the key, we're told—and we are so out of touch with our own bodies that we just keep on pushing. We strain and extend our reach, and we have no idea if the goal is in alignment, or out of alignment, with our capability or fitness or needs.

So, why am I leading you into the next section of this book with the stories of two failed business ventures and an entrepreneur who has got to where she wants to be despite the struggle of the journey?

The point isn't that Susannah's, or Lauren's, or my ventures failed. It's not that the ventures were incredibly hard-going. The point is what happened for each of us inside our heads when things didn't go to plan. Susannah and Lauren were trying to 'go big' in life and business. That was my goal too! I have seen this happen countless times with the women entrepreneurs I have met and worked with.

You're feeling amazing about your big vision and starting to execute it.

But you get hit with a setback that makes you question everything. It's almost like you've been driving down the road as your Next Level Self, but without getting ready for the journey and just assuming that your Plan A will fall into place. And when it does, you'll make a ton of money!

So when mindset whiplash kicks in, you feel your bravery and boldness quickly turn to deep, paralyzing fear. And suddenly your Next Level Self becomes your Inner Child, and things are getting way out of control. We'll be talking more about the Inner Child in the next chapter, but she is not the part of you who should be driving the car on your journey to more! She feels small and scared in the face of danger, but she is now the one driving the car, making all the wrong interpretations and honestly this IS terrifying. She is too young to drive! She doesn't understand what she is looking at or feeling, and it is like all the confidence you had about your big vision has just evaporated right in front of you.

If you don't know to expect it, mindset whiplash will make you want to stop the car and turn around to go home. It will make you feel like you were wrong to ever set out, and that you now regret all the big, bold steps you took. It's natural to shrink back after mindset whiplash. To tell yourself you've learned your lesson. No more big ambitions. The End. It can make us feel even more like too much, and like we can't trust our instincts and drive for more. It can also make us force ourselves forward, just as blind to the aligned path we should be on, but determined to not quit and not back down. It is like driving into a storm, and we make ourselves do it every day calling it business growth and forward progress.

Here's what I've found to be true. If you feel like too much, even if you say you are quitting your business—even if you actually do quit—it isn't the end because that little spark of an idea is still calling out to you. Maybe you're reading this, and you've never successfully found your 'more'. Maybe you've had a few failed attempts at starting the journey and now you're realizing you're gearing up for a new attempt, but you feel like, *What's the point because it always fails?*

I have to tell you—if you've had disappointments like this, if you feel like you're too much, you *need* to go on this journey. There's a part of you that will not find rest until you find your ultimate 'more', and you deserve to find peak fulfillment as much as the next person.

So how do you actually do that? Well I'm glad you asked, because in Part Two I'm sharing the framework of what it looks like to look for your 'more' in practical terms.

Over the next three chapters we are going to explore the 3-step process we need to follow that will help identify what your 'more' looks like, and not just be able to articulate it but to bring it into being. I call it *Connecting, Dealing and Feeling*.

Here are the three steps:

1. We Connect to Abundance.
2. We Deal with the Inner Critic.
3. We Feel for Seven Figure Aligned Actions.

These three little steps are the *easiest hardest* thing you will ever do, but when you commit to being consistent with all three at each stage of your journey to 'more', it means you can hold space for the visions of your highest self without experiencing the mindset whiplash that can derail us on the journey.

It's the powerful roadmap you need to help you on your journey to 'more', and I'm going to show you how to navigate it without getting derailed.

Let's dive in!

6 Connect to Abundance

In this chapter, we are going to lean into our first step of *Connecting, Dealing and Feeling*—Connecting to Abundance. But what does that mean, and why is it important?

Have you ever had the experience of scrolling through your LinkedIn feed only to notice someone who has a business that seems kind of similar to yours, only it feels like they are doing everything so much better? One minute ago, you were feeling fairly confident about your business prospects, but suddenly you are thrown into doubt and fear.

It's an experience that you've likely had before and can relate to, but you may not have connected the dots on why it feels the way it does. Welcome to a problem you may never have realized you have—scarcity!

So here's what's on the agenda for this chapter. We're going to explore what scarcity is, and the simple, feel-good antidote that is abundance. We're then going to look at the different 'parts' of us that show up when we're wrestling with decisions in business, and focus on how to summon the ones that can help instead of hinder our progress.

Hello Scarcity, My Old Friend

You might not realize it, but it is incredibly likely that up to this point in your life, your brain has been dominated by 'scarcity beliefs'. The fear that other people will steal what is yours. The fear that money and resources will run out. The belief that everything has to be hard, and that success can only be yours if you pay a heavy price for it. The belief that this world is defined by there not being enough, and we need to compete and win at all costs. Even if you feel expansive and bold right now, scarcity beliefs are often lurking ready to find us.

Believing the world is all about scarcity affects us in a number of ways—it leads to under-investment in your business as it grows, and a failure to see and act on opportunities that leaves countless amounts of money on the table and creates so. much. unnecessary. gut-wrenching. fear on the journey. And straightaway, there's also a link here between scarcity and trauma because not only does trauma cause our body and brain to be rewired to see the world as threatening and unsafe, it follows logically that if the world is like this, scarcity will seem more 'true' to us than abundance. Scarcity can often feel safe because it is familiar, and we know what it is and where we are with it.

Even though we may have been raised to see the world through a scarcity lens—*eat everything on your plate, there are starving children in Africa, don't waste! be careful! work hard!* —it doesn't just affect the way we see the world. It affects the way we see ourselves. Even feeling like or being told we are too much is a scarcity belief. Because if we are too much, that immediately implies we are asking for more than our fair share of attention or nurture. *There's not enough—you're taking too much!*

And so it becomes mission critical that we learn to look through the lens of abundance instead. And like putting on a new pair of glasses, choosing to view the world and our businesses, and more than that, our whole lives, in the context of *abundance* instead of scarcity CHANGES EVERYTHING.

Switching Scarcity for Abundance

Many entrepreneurs start their businesses with scarcity beliefs at the forefront, but as you start down the road of entrepreneurship, it is not long before you start to realize that *business growth* and *scarcity beliefs* simply cannot co-exist. We cannot create abundance in our businesses if we are determined to believe that the world is all about scarcity. Remember our story from the start of this chapter, of seeing someone else's social media posts and suddenly finding ourselves coming up short?

It is really important to notice where our brains go in those moments—because all too often, the scarcity lens is right there, lurking in the shadows to show us the negative perspective. *OMG. She looks so much more professional than you. Look how great her skin is! And she has more followers! And look at all those people she knows! Everyone is going to work with her and not with you! I'm so depressed! I may as well give up now!*

Whereas when we can look at this through an abundance lens, we get a completely different picture: *Wow, I love what she is doing with her business and look at those brand photos! So professional! I wonder if she would be open to collaborating together because I bet there are people in my network who would be a fit for her and probably also people in her network who might be a fit for me—there's enough clients for all of us so I'm going to reach out and see if we can help one another.*

Can you feel the difference? And, I mean, can you FEEL the difference?

It's an important awareness for us to gain because when we realize that we have the choice over whether we wear the 'scarcity glasses' or the 'abundance glasses', it is such a powerful uplevel. It's that same realization we already saw back in Chapter 4—*you are at choice*. How we choose to see the world is up to us. And our internal messaging can completely shift when we choose abundance instead of scarcity.

Flipping the Script

So how can we define abundance? It is quite literally taking our scarcity beliefs and flipping them into the opposite meaning.

The fear that other people will steal what is yours can become—*"I possess an unlimited ability to create more."*

The fear that money and resources will run out can become—*"Money can never run out. I have access to everything I need and I always will."*

The belief that everything has to be hard, and that success can only be yours if you pay a heavy price for it can become— *"I can allow this to be easy."*

The belief that this world is defined by there not being enough, and we need to compete and win at all costs can become— *"I choose collaboration over competition"* (which incidentally is one of my favorite phrases!). Exploring the ways we can help one another succeed, rather than fearing this person or company will take what I already have.

If you are ever struggling to know how to shift a scarcity belief into abundance, I'd love to share a principle that I teach my clients, and that is—we need to make it safe and fun. This applies to our business activities, particularly when we are looking at business growth and how to go outside of our comfort zone without experiencing mindset whiplash, but it also applies to our lives outside of our businesses. We need it to be safe, so we are free to soar and lean into the energy of our Higher Self, and we need it to be fun so that our natural energy bubbles up and creates the momentum we are looking for. And making things safe and fun is such an important principle that really links in to scarcity and abundance because abundance is fundamentally about safety, whereas scarcity is always focused on fear and lack of safety.

If you have a scarcity belief, maybe you're looking at your business bank balance and it feels like it's lower than you would ideally like, and you're tempted to panic and tell yourself— *"I'm running out of money!"* Ask yourself, instead of falling down a rabbit hole of fear, what would make this feel safe and fun? You can flip this scarcity belief to abundance— *"There is always more money. I can easily attract more. I know how to do this."* It's amazing when I do this exercise with clients how quickly they'll say, *"Oh, yes! I forgot—I have a year's worth of living and business expenses sitting in my savings account."*

It's amazing the things we 'forget' when scarcity kicks in! Because like with trauma, our scarcity beliefs overtake everything we can see around us when they kick in—we are reacting to things that are not happening.

You know you've hit the right note with reframing your scarcity as abundance when you feel the tension disappear—your sense of *fear* has switched to *safety.*

"Who is speaking?"

Because the world around us—people, the news and social media, capitalism, even your own brain—is so wired around scarcity, one of the most important things we need to do as we ascertain what our 'more' is, is to learn to discern our own intuition around what abundance looks like. It's another one of those situations where entrepreneurship is a path of one, and we sometimes need to be ready to pull away from the pack in order to discern what is truly in alignment for us.

A really helpful tool in this exercise is starting to ask ourselves, *when I had that thought, who was speaking?*

We so often receive our internal monologue as fact, and we don't realize that it is the voice of our subconscious mind, and that actually, it can be really wrong about all kinds of things. We will dig into this more in Chapter 7 but for now, I want to explore the idea that we typically get a range of voices showing up internally, also called 'Parts'.[28] Here are some examples I'm going to illustrate for you to help our understanding of what these voices are and how they show up for us.

1. The Dissociated Self
2. The Inner Critic
3. The Inner Child
4. The Higher Self

1. The Dissociated Self

As we have already touched on in Chapter 3, the Dissociated Self is in a state of perpetual numbness. It is often a switched-off state, where we aren't pushing on any doors that might have big emotions behind them. So, we do life without pushing on those doors.

As I already shared, after I went through burnout, I didn't know how to feel my feelings or even answer the question *"How are you?"*. And I often find with my clients that when we first work together, while we are discussing a concept or strategy, I will ask *"How does that feel?"* Initially, often, they will blink and say, *"It feels fine"* or *"Yes, good, thank you, Jessica."* They might show some mild irritation at what seems like such a pointless question. They may even think their coach is showing a bit of neediness!

If we believe that our feelings don't matter, or we are working to suppress our feelings, it follows that it becomes kind of dumb to ask about it. But I'm not asking for an ego boost in that moment, or looking for their feedback. I'm encouraging them to check in with themselves and feel for the answer.

"It feels fine" is not an adequate answer, because I want to know what they feel specifically and where in their body they feel it. This can be a challenge when we first start to make this kind of enquiry of ourselves, but the good news is that over time, it becomes a powerful language we can speak with ourselves. If you don't know what to do in a situation, your Dissociated Self might tell you *"I don't know what to do"*. And you'll hear no emotion or intonation in her voice. Everything is flat and disconnected.

But as we learn to recognize the body sensations that come up while we are exploring difficult decisions—maybe a sudden tension in your shoulders, or a flicker of excitement in your gut—this becomes a powerful way for us to realize that we know exactly what to do.

So, if you're feeling flat, numb and the only response echoing around inside your head is *"I don't know"*, it's likely that the voice speaking is your Dissociated Self. There can be situations where your "I don't know" is your Inner Child, as we'll see in a moment, but the Dissociated Self is flat and unemotional, whereas the Inner Child often brings her own firework show of emotions and turbulence.

2. The Inner Critic

The Inner Critic is the version of us who loves to poke holes in our brilliant ideas. It is our Inner Critic who is cruel, spiteful, vindictive, and never lets us forget when we've got something wrong or made a mistake. It is your Inner Critic who loves to tell you you are too much! He or she tries to grab the steering wheel of life and business when they sense danger. But it's like a faulty 'check engine' light on your dashboard because it also shows up when there is no inherent danger.

As we've already explored in Chapter 4, often we find that exposure to trauma means we are reacting to things that aren't still happening. And to stop them from ever happening again, we develop a strict set of rules we believe we need to live by in order to stay safe. The Inner Critic polices these rules and loves to get loud when you're in danger of breaking them. It's not about actually being in danger, it's about protecting your Inner Critic's strict set of rules at all costs.

It is a really powerful tool if you can develop an awareness that your Inner Critic has grabbed the mic internally. We will be zeroing in on how to deal with the Inner Critic in Chapter 7, but for now, it's enough to have the realization that he or she is speaking.

3. The Inner Child

Your Inner Child can get really loud when you start doing expansive growth work. In fact, whenever you feel fear or scarcity it can be a sign that your Inner Child is activated. The Inner Critic can summon the Inner Child, because often when we feel criticized, we revert to a childlike state internally. Ever wondered why that difficult client leaves you feeling either like you want to have a full-blown tantrum or run away and hide in a cupboard after a tense meeting? This is one of the specialties of the Inner Child.

Our Inner Child can give us some powerful clues about what our authentic self is like, and what we truly want. She also has some valuable insights about what needs were not met for us in childhood—she often craves safety and acceptance. But it's helpful to understand if your Inner Child is speaking for you internally, because, although she feels big feelings, she does not know how to hold adult emotions. She cannot perceive complexity and jumps to conclusions, often blaming herself for things she had no influence over, such as the emotions of the adults around her or sequences of events that had nothing to do with her.

A variant on the Inner Child is the Inner Teenager, and while the Inner Child has a predilection to fear, the Inner Teenager is often the one who feels a lot of anger and wants to smash things or take reckless action.

Both need love, acceptance and careful handling. And when you can recognize that your Inner Child or Inner Teenager are speaking, there are some really powerful soothing techniques that can bring your inner adult to the fore again.

4. The Higher Self

While the Dissociated Self and the Inner Critic are voices we want to be aware of so we can shift out of them, and the Inner Child and Inner Teenager are a part of us we might want to soothe, the Higher Self is a *bona fide* voice we can welcome.

Your Higher Self is your highest, most energized self. She can feel the future and the future is in full technicolor. She has perfect clarity. She sees the path ahead and she knows it is going to be easy. She speaks and understands the language of abundance. More than that—she knows it is already done. There is no doubt. There is only excitement and deep certainty. Your Higher Self cannot be moved. She is the version of you who is the most 'too much' and yet is not too much at all because she has found the right place and outlet for her gifts.

In the work I do with my clients, we often tap into a version of the Higher Self we call the Seven Figure Self, which is the future 'business' version of them who has already achieved the Seven Figure revenue goal they dream of achieving. Some of my clients already have eight figure selves or nine figure selves. It's a really powerful exercise to tap into this version of you. This future self, who already has the things you currently dream of. Sometimes it's the aesthetics—the house, the car, the clothes, the things. Sometimes it's the high-level clients, the accolades, the key note speaking opportunities or the TV appearances. Sometimes it's the emotional wellbeing, the completion of healing work. The confidence, the positivity, the sense of certainty and of achievement. There's no reason why it can't be all of these things!

Once you begin your journey of personal growth, you are constantly evolving from one version of yourself to the next. This is why sometimes we might talk about your Next Level Self, and sometimes we might talk about your Seven Figure Self. Your Next Level Self is marking milestones on the journey to seven figures. Your Seven Figure Self is the version of you who has already got there! Both are versions of the Higher Self, and we can use any or all of these terms interchangeably. Sometimes we will feel this growth happening and see that each year we are uplevelling again and again. Sometimes like a snake shedding its skin, we feel the uplevelling happen almost in a frenzy over the space of a few weeks or a few months. Our vision keeps getting bigger. And as we established in Chapter 3, this brings the exhilaration of personal growth but also the sadness of saying goodbye to the old self we are letting go of. It's all part of the process of growth, letting go of what we have grown past and stepping into the version of us that is opening up in front.

So how can we truly connect to abundance when we are exploring what our 'more' looks like and what the path to greater fulfillment will be?

Summoning your Higher Self is a really helpful way to do this, but we can connect to abundance any time we choose. It's important because when we are channeling our Higher Self, we are in that energetic place where everything feels easy, and we are open to uplevelling. It feels like there are no bad ideas and we feel certain that everything we're dreaming up will be a roaring success.

If you are trying to make some difficult decisions in your business—*should you change your service offering? Should you look to evolve your team structure? Should you hire that new supplier? Should you fire a legacy client?*—knowing who is speaking internally for you as you make that decision has a huge impact on the outcome of that decision.

The different voices have distinct ways of interacting as we mull things over, often causing the decision-making process to feel agonizing and impossible to reach consensus on. The Dissociated Self shrugs and pushes us to defer the situation. The Inner Critic casts doubt on our plans and triggers shame so that we will stay home and stay safe. The Inner Child feels deep fear and doubts every option, while our Inner Teenager often wants to burn it all to the ground.

Our Higher Self, or Seven Figure Self, is the one who can whisper what 'next level' looks like, and it is a perspective that we often need to most engage with, and yet it can be so easily drowned out by the rabble.

So how do we connect to abundance at those critical crossroads moments?

How to Summon Your Higher Self

When we are connecting to abundance, your Higher Self or Seven Figure Self is a perfect ally to summon. And there is no 'one way' to achieve this.

Sometimes it happens effortlessly. You might be casually day dreaming, or just feeling really good and like you can really feel everything lining up exactly the way you want it to in your business.

Sometimes, our Higher Self appears when we are having a 'next level' experience. Maybe you just won an award or a big contract. I actually think travel can be a really powerful experience that summons our Higher Self, especially when it involves air travel. You are literally transcending your normal day-to-day life and flying high above the rest of the world. Maybe you find it happening when you're eating at a restaurant you have always wanted to go to, or having a luxury spa day, or experiencing high fulfillment through quality relationships with your spouse, family, kids, or friends. You can feel it through your work—maybe you have received recognition from your peers or your industry, or a standing ovation to a keynote you have given.

Whenever you feel that amazing expansive feeling that actually everything is going brilliantly, and everything you want to achieve feels easy and within reach—that is a great indicator that your Higher Self has appeared.

In my work with my clients, we often map out the specifics of who their Seven Figure Self is. Or if that feels too daunting, we start with their 'Next Level Self', knowing there may be several 'next levels' before the Seven Figure Self feels like the next step.

And we get specific about:

- *Who she is*
- *What she does*
- *Who she knows*
- *Where she lives*
- *Where she travels*
- *What she earns*
- *What she has*
- *What she knows*

We want to document as many details as we can because over the next few months it is always the case that the items on this list start to get ticked off as you grow into your next version. I used to love doing this as a mind map on huge paper, sticking it to my office wall and ticking off each thing as it happens, but I discovered last year that one of my clients has a 'whiteboard wall' in her office and it inspired me to do the same. It feels so good to grab a marker and get really big and creative. Plus, writing on a wall—what a treat for your Inner Child!

Another technique I like to use with my clients is to create an abundance 'anchor' together. We feel into how abundance is showing up for us internally, where the feeling of abundance appears in our bodies, what colors and images we get. It could be a magical fountain, or the ocean, or a rainbow, or a luxury bathroom. And then they decide on a simple action they will take to 'anchor' this feeling, maybe a posture they can take or a specific motion they can make, so they can return to the feel of abundance whenever they need to. I am always amazed at how creative these actions end up being, from printing an image to stick above your desk, to creating poses and postures, to going out and buying a specific item, or even to commissioning a painting!

We might also create a question for me to ask them, or for them to ask themselves to remind them to use the perspective of abundance when they are tempted to default to scarcity. My husband accidentally created a great one for me. I was feeling stressed about how many appointments I should book to maintain my eyelash extensions that month (yup, I heard it!). I was trying to decide if I wanted a two-week, or a three-week infill appointment. And I think he was even slightly pulling my leg in the moment, but it provided exactly what I needed. He asked, *"What does abundance look like in this situation?"* As soon as he said it, I knew exactly what to do—I needed to ask if they could do me a weekly infill. The salon said yes, and my eyelashes have felt abundant ever since!

Of course, this is a trivial example compared to making wide-ranging changes to your business, but, in my experience, when we can really nail the small decisions we know how to make the big decisions when they come along.

Connecting to abundance and embodying our Seven Figure Self is like flipping on the light switch in a dark room and realizing that clarity is all around us. It is the lens we need to look through so that we can be most connected to the path to greater fulfillment and more than that, peak fulfillment.

So, I would love to encourage you to make this a regular practice when you think about your business and what peak fulfillment would look like for you. No dream is too big or too small. Simply notice—what is your soul sending you? What image keeps coming up time and time again? For one of my clients, it was taking the trip of a lifetime. For another, it was standing on a stage giving a keynote at the top conference in her industry. For another, it was having all her debts paid and a fully funded retirement.

It is essential that we devote proper time at regular intervals to sit with our thoughts and reflections and see if there is a bigger version out there opening up in front of us.

For me, a really important part of my daily routine is walking outdoors with my dog. She is a very bouncy cockerpoo and loves to explore. And this time every day gives me the space to think and reflect about my business but also about what is going on for each of my clients. A lot of my content ideas come up during this time. I actually wrote the first version of the introduction to this book while I was on a dog walk, typing frantically on my phone with one thumb while I held the dog lead and a dog poop bag in the other!

But business retreats, or even personal retreats, can also be really powerful for getting us out of our day-to-day routines and creating space for powerful, abundant thinking. I host business retreats for my Seven Figures Club program ladies several times a year, and it is always a wonderfully expansive uplevel experience!

When we can feel abundance in our bodies, we can hold space for a bigger vision in our minds. We need to allow it time and space to become fully formed so that we know we will feel that oh-so-satisfying sense of fulfillment when we have executed it. And to help you connect to abundance—I've created a special guided meditation called Opening Up To Abundance. You can download it for free from jessicafearnley.com/bonus—along with the other exclusive book bonuses!

Is It Big Enough?

A question we always need to be asking ourselves is, is this vision big enough?

If it isn't big enough, if we rush to execution before allowing the idea to become fully formed, it won't feel magical to achieve it. I have had clients who execute every line of their business plan for the year but feel flat and discouraged when they realize—it was achievable but it wasn't enough. Or clients who have the spark of an idea for some really exciting, next-level, super-expansive moves in their business, but allow the pressure of 'how' to creep in and shrink it all down.

We have to be really disciplined so we don't make it smaller at every stage. Our internal voices might be pushing us to contract, play safe, aim low. Maybe it's a new offer that is slightly terrifying to start pitching. Maybe it's a high-profile event or an industry conference that will take some courage to pull off. When we listen to our internal voices and decide in advance what the outcome is going to be, and then make all the wrong assumptions, we're just setting ourselves up for disappointment all over again.

You need to allow the idea to become fully formed and FEEL into it.

And this last part—feeling our way into an idea—is something that Western education and corporate life in no way prepares us for. We have to ask ourselves, what feels abundant in this moment? What would it feel like if your cup was overflowing and like everything you touch turns to gold and you can have anything you want because you are in touch with the universe and receiving divine downloads of the purpose and the place in the world that you are meant to take up? What would you do if THAT were true?

This is what it means to connect to abundance and channel your Higher Self. And this is a really important thing that I teach my clients to do, because it's not enough to know we need to NOT channel our Dissociated Self or our Inner Critic. If you *don't* do stuff, you end up with nothing. You need to positively connect to abundance and take action as your Higher Self, your Seven Figure Self.

Just say you are planning a conference for your industry, that will be packed with your ideal clients and will create an abundance of new leads for your business—after all, they say if you can't find the event you want to attend it's a sign you should create one, right?

Your Dissociated Self will not nurture this idea and make it bigger. This version of you has a tendency towards inaction and will probably just shrug and consign the idea to the pile of "stuff I thought about but never did".

Your Inner Critic will not nurture this idea. They will sabotage it, make it smaller—and worse, make you feel stupid for even entertaining it for a moment.

Your Inner Child might find this idea enchanting but turns and flees at the first bump in the road.

But your Higher Self will be able to nurture the idea. To allow it to become bigger, not smaller. To fix issues as they arise and be resourceful.

What if we looked for sponsorship?

What if we invited 100 people not 10, or 1,000 people not 100.

Oh wait, the biggest thought leader in my field is on a book tour that month. They would absolutely say yes to the keynote at the conference.

And when the idea is big enough, you will know because you will get the impulse to act AND, when you do it, it will feel like the easiest thing you ever did.

Value Over Volume

But it's not about just making it big for the sake of being big. The goal with this isn't size, it's alignment.

One of the big principles I teach to my clients is what I call Value over Volume. This is where we grow a business not by volume—adding in lots more clients and scaling a big team so suddenly there's all kinds of friction, and profits aren't increasing—there's just more turnover and costs.

Instead, we opt for growth through value. Serving at your highest level and creating high ticket consulting offers so you can do the maximum in revenue with the simplest of business models. Maximum gain, minimum effort.

For years I have made, if I'm being frank, a ton more money than the average coach because I love to do really deep work and I charge what my coaching is worth based on the results my clients get. I don't just help my clients feel good about themselves and their mission and purpose. I also help them increase their revenue by hundreds of thousands of dollars, and we do it by prioritizing value over volume. This means that they don't have to add 100 new clients to grow their consulting business to seven figures, or hire 20 new consultants to help make it happen. It means that they can take the simplest of actions and get huge revenue returns. Put up their prices. Onboard 2-3 new clients. Hire an Operations Manager.

When you are connected to your Dissociated Self or your Inner Critic, it feels like all progress is impossible. When you are connected to your Seven Figure Self, it all feels so clear! You don't need a huge business empire. Like we explored in Chapter 5, you can have a seven figure consulting business with 2-10 clients—IF you leverage value instead of volume.

As we've seen, your Higher Self is the critical piece of the puzzle for making your too much feel like just the right amount. It's the North Star you can follow to get to your 'more'. But Connecting to Abundance can open us up to the dreaded mindset whiplash, which makes us want to abandon our big vision! Don't forget to access your free guided meditation by visiting jessicafearnley.com/bonus.

So how can you equip yourself to hold onto abundance and not get spooked when mindset whiplash comes to visit? In the next chapter we are going to do just that—by exploring the second step of my *Connecting, Dealing and Feeling* framework, and learning how to deal with the Inner Critic.

See you there!

CHAPTER SUMMARY

» Hello Scarcity, My Old Friend
» Switching Scarcity for Abundance
» Flipping the Script
» "Who is speaking?"
» How to Summon Your Higher Self
» Is It Big Enough?
» Value Over Volume

7 Dealing with the Inner Critic

In Chapter 6 we explored what it means to Connect to Abundance and how we can summon our Higher Self, or our Seven Figure Self.

Job done, right? Not quite yet. Our second step of *Connecting, Dealing and Feeling*—Dealing with the Inner Critic—is essential for us to know about so we can avoid the dreaded mindset whiplash that occurs when we get really bold and expansive. If you remember, mindset whiplash can hit when we create space for the vision of our Higher Self but get spooked the moment we start taking the actions to turn that dream of ours into reality. Remember Susannah and her failed launch, Lauren and her big rebrand, and my story of throwing myself repeatedly at the brick wall? I'm going to show you how to prevent this from happening to you in your journey to 'more.' Because no one loves to make you feel like too much—or fear that you are not enough—quite as much as your Inner Critic!

In this chapter we are going to do a quick deep dive into how to deal with your Inner Critic, the voice that is all too ready to belittle and criticize our expansive plans. We are going to discover the fatal flaw of your Inner Critic (because they are very good at concealing it), what we can do to stop them from stomping all over your business plans, and how we can practice this safely when your Inner Critic is also your Inner Child.

In my previous chapter I showed how the Inner Critic is the version of us who loves to poke holes in our brilliant ideas. He or she can be spectacularly harsh towards us, whispering—or even shouting—the most cruel, spiteful and vindictive things to us. They never let us forget when we've got something wrong or made a mistake.

But who is this Inner Critic?

It could be that your Inner Critic doesn't speak with 'your' voice at all. It could be that he or she is a completely different entity from you. It could have its roots in the critical voice of someone in your life, a critical parent or family member. Or maybe even a teacher from your school or university. A former boss or colleague. I know for a while mine felt like it spoke in the same tone as the school bully who went through a phase of finding a lot of the things I did and said to be annoying when we were middle-school teenagers. We can carry critical voices with us for a long time, but however much this critical voice may have hurt you in the past, you don't need to carry it with you any longer. You don't need to carry it in the same way that you may have carried it up to now, and I'm going to show you a neat tip for neutralizing its sting.

One of the exercises I love to do with clients is to get them to visualize their Inner Critic and create a character or avatar for them—the quirkier and sillier the better. It never fails to amaze me how powerful a tool this can be. Not only does it help you to unleash your creativity, it's a brilliant way to immediately receive the voice of your Inner Critic differently. Maybe you're reading this and thinking, *isn't that the worst thing you could do, Jessica? Why would you want to encourage your clients to pay more attention to this voice when surely, they should be giving it less attention?*

But the thing is—we want to understand a little more about your Inner Critic and how it manifests for you so that we can notice who it is, where it likely came from, and what you can do each time it appears. My clients have made the most wonderfully imaginative visualizations about their Inner Critic and the specific character or form it takes. It might be a negative energy. It might be a person from their life, or a former part of their life. It might be a character from TV or a movie.

And once we have identified this voice, we create a visualization for how they want to deal with it. The days of taking the voice of your Inner Critic at face value are over, my friend! There are no rules about how this needs to be done. We are essentially asking the question—now that you've noticed this character is showing up and saying these things, how do you feel you want to respond? Answers range from politely sending him or her away, to making them walk the plank, to telling them to shut up, to even acting out shooting them in the face with a make-believe shot gun! It can be surprisingly satisfying to silence your Inner Critic!

The Secret Your Inner Critic Doesn't Want You to Know

It isn't just about creating a character and visualizing a response that shuts them down though. It is a really valuable exercise to develop your awareness of when your Inner Critic appears. Because when you realize it's your Inner Critic speaking, you become aware your brain may not be processing true facts or assessing risk in a balanced way. We always assume our thoughts are facts and the voice in our head only speaks the truth, but this is far from being the case! I said in the last chapter that your Inner Critic loves to show up and try to grab the steering wheel of life and business when they sense danger. But the problem is—your Inner Critic is not able to sense real danger. He, or she, is like a faulty 'check engine' light on the dashboard. You will find them showing up when there is no actual danger, which is a problem because it leads to us feeling conflicted or anxious where there is no reason to be.

And this is at the heart of the biggest secret about your Inner Critic—a secret that your Inner Critic is banking on you not knowing. Ready to hear it?

The thing that most people in the world never realize is that your Inner Critic doesn't have access to any information than you don't already have. They don't have any more information that you do—and they are often working on less. Why? Because so many of the 'alternative facts' that your Inner Critic serves up are based on faulty information, for example, a belief from your childhood that you were to blame for something that as an adult you now realize there is no way you could be responsible for. This could be your parents' unhappy marriage, a relative's illness or death, adult relatives not getting on, lack of money at home, or some other external stressor present during your childhood.

It is so tempting to feel like your Inner Critic has the inside track, or they know how things are going to play out. I often work on this with clients who seem to believe they have developed an ability to predict the future—for example, what people will say or do in advance of an actual event, or how a sales conversation will turn out. It's especially important to do this work when you find yourself constantly predicting negative outcomes. We all do this from time to time, but turning something you are excited about into a lose-lose situation is one of your Inner Critic's favorite games.

The game looks like this:

I won't reach out to that potential client—they don't want to hear from me.

I better not increase my prices, no one will pay this.

I've sent the proposal, but I can't see them accepting it.

They've said yes, but I don't think the work is actually going to go forward. Even if it does, I won't be able to resource the project and I'll end up having to do all this work myself.

Like you're suddenly playing the world's tiniest, saddest violin. *There's no point trying,* we say to ourselves, *because I already know what the outcome is going to be and it won't work out.*

Here's the thing though—and I bet you already know this. Friend, you don't have the ability to predict the future. The feeling that you know what will happen is a combination of your Inner Critic and possibly also the trauma in your backstory. One of my biggest breakthroughs in my own coaching journey was making the realization of exactly this—my tendency towards hypervigilance makes me feel as if I have the power to predict the future and prevent bad things from happening. But I don't. In fact to hammer this point home, I have a post-it note stuck to my office computer screen. It says, "*Anything can happen!*" with a smiley face to remind me that this is a good thing! I've even decorated it with some of the stars from my kids' reward charts (although for the record, part of the reason I have so many star stickers lying around is because I have not done a good job of being consistent with reward charts!)

Because we don't have the ability to predict the future, it makes sense that we should keep ourselves open for any and every possibility—after all, anything can happen! And when our Inner Critic tempts us to play the game of negative predictions about meetings and decisions and sales calls, we need to remember this. And to see the expansiveness of what this means for us. Because for us as entrepreneurs, of all the people on the planet WE are the ones most able to change the negative story you might have been telling yourself into a success story. Don't forget this. We are not power*less*, we are power*ful*.

And this is a brilliant way to contradict your Inner Critic in those moments when it can feel like we are totally at the mercy of their negative predictions and gloomy forecasts. Remember, your Inner Critic doesn't have access to any information that you don't also have. There is no inside track, or secret wisdom to be found.

More than this, and are you ready to have your mind blown? You may have seen the online meme *"Tell the negative committee that meets inside your head to sit down and shut up"*. I want to take this a step further and remind you that, actually, the negative committee inside your head doesn't even exist. It's not just that they are passing off wrong information as fact. There isn't even a committee. The voice does not even exist. It is a figment of your subconscious mind.

So why are we listening to something so ridiculous?

Worse than that, why are we listening and failing to recognize that it is selling us fake news?

Last year I was in the middle of a bathroom renovation project being done at home. We had moved out of our house for a couple of weeks to give the contractors the space they needed to complete the work, and, although it had seemed like it would be super simple when we were planning it, I found those two weeks were rather more stretching than I had anticipated.

One of the things I like to do for self-care (and something that has helped immeasurably with trauma recovery for me) is a weekly full body massage. And while my bathroom project was going on, I booked in for a massage. During my time on the table I felt all my tension over bathroom tiles and pipework and project scope creep melting away. After the massage had finished, I went to grab my beanie hat from my bag only to realize that I'd forgotten it at home. So I had no choice but to leave the salon with my short hair practically standing on end. I tried to smooth it down while I got changed, but it was somehow simultaneously oily AND frizzy, and would not be flattened! I walked down the street back to my car feeling good from the massage, but also a little self conscious. And as I opened the car door, I caught a view of my reflection and couldn't help but feel embarrassed. "*Wow, Jessica*", I said to myself. "*Everyone is looking at you and thinking you must be out of your mind to be walking around looking like this."*

Thoughts like this aren't a new thing to me. I have spent a lot of my life indulging in self hatred and my Inner Critic, even now, can be vicious. But all of a sudden, something new happened. I don't know why, but in that moment I looked up the street and I looked down the street, and replayed the thought:

"Everyone is looking at you." Honestly, there was literally no one in the street. No one in their front yard or at a window. I was by myself in the street.

"Thinking you must be out of your mind." And I realized—not only was it untrue that everyone was looking at me and thinking really mean things about me, but the voice that asserted these 'facts' so confidently DOES NOT EVEN EXIST.

I suddenly found myself talking back to my Inner Critic. *"I'm sorry, Inner Critic,"* (and isn't that the most wonderfully British thing, because of course I wasn't sorry but it is deeply embedded within the British psyche to say sorry on all occasions—this is something that causes my American clients to make fun of me often), *"I'm sorry, Inner Critic, but you don't even exist, so you don't get a say!"* Against that background, it actually makes sense to disregard that opinion, right?!

And here's the important part—when we have defused the Inner Critic, we don't just want to remove the negative thought or belief, we are ready to lay a new, true thought or belief in its place. We are creating a new pathway for your brain to follow instead now that it knows the old belief is false. And in that moment, my intuition told me powerfully, *"Hello?! It's a Friday morning and not only are you not at work like most of the people you know, you just spent the last hour getting a massage. If we are talking about living your best life, I think you just did it!"*

Can you feel how much more empowering it is when we can stop falling for our own fake news? And let me tell you, this moment did not happen in a vacuum. This ability to spot the voice, doubt the content AND remember that it is not coming from a place of truth, or of even existing at all, plus replacing it with something better, is something that becomes possible when we do the work of dealing with our Inner Critic.

Dealing with our Inner Critic is important work. So how do we do it? How can we set up the conditions that help us to spot the voice, doubt the voice, disprove it and replace it with something better?

Turning Down the Volume

I'm going to share an exercise that I often do with clients that really helps you to find a more empowered story in those moments where the Inner Critic is biting hard. I've even created you a handy printable that will help. Go to jessicafearnley.com/bonus and download it.

Here's what you do. Using my handy printable, or a sheet of blank paper if you prefer, you're going to grab a black pen and list out every limiting belief your Inner Critic has to throw at you in this moment. Leave a line between each one (you'll see why in a minute!) But really allow this voice to speak. This might sound counterintuitive because, again, are we really sure we want to allow a putrid fountain of accusations to flow from your Inner Critic? Yes, he or she possesses the meanest, most spiteful voice you'll likely hear. But something powerful happens when we stop suppressing this voice and start exploring the validity of what it is saying to us.

When we are trying to suppress this voice, it is like tuning into a negativity radio station that we have playing on low volume all the time. Sometimes it is like a battle internally where the voice of your Inner Critic keeps getting louder and louder, and you keep diving for the volume control knob to turn it down again. Your Inner Critic responds by turning it up and the relentless conflict between them and you feels completely exhausting.

Ever wondered why it can be so bone-shatteringly tiring to be an entrepreneur? If you haven't managed to take back control of the dial, fighting this battle all the time will drain your energy faster than a high-powered app running in the background drains your device battery.

And it's not just that your Inner Critic creates noise—it often seems like he or she is making a convincing argument, so we need to do more than just try to keep turning the volume down. We need to turn it off completely, but that doesn't happen in the way you might expect. We need to engage with what this fake news radio station keeps broadcasting inside your brain, because that is the real chink in its armor.

First Step—Let Your Inner Critic Speak

So, on a blank sheet of paper, list out each limiting belief your Inner Critic is throwing at you, leaving a blank line between each one. And don't worry about how bad or dark and twisty this list of limiting beliefs looks when it's all written down. This is a great way to detox your brain! You might find that it feels hard at first, but I promise you that once you get going, you'll find the limiting beliefs flooding out. We often only have half a thought, and this process is all about letting the full thought out so we know what we are dealing with, and in a moment, we can find a way to counter it using our rational mind.

You might find these kinds of things coming up:

- *You have failed at everything you have ever done.*
- *You aren't good at making money.*
- *You don't have a clue what you're doing.*
- *No one will buy this.*
- *You should have stayed in your corporate job.*

And even things like:

- *You're such a loser.*
- *You are terrible with money.*
- *You're a failure.*

I have done this exercise myself and with groups of women in my programs and workshops many, many times. My clients are highly experienced, elite women entrepreneurs and consultants. It is hard to believe that they would harbor any self-doubt or self-criticism, but I have seen time and time again just how creative our brains can be at conjuring negative and limiting beliefs about who we are and what we are trying to do in our businesses.

These beliefs are absolutely the kinds of things that look horrific written down in a list. As the adage goes, you wouldn't tolerate someone saying it to a friend, so why say it to yourself? We absolutely need to break the cycle of allowing your brain to say it to you on repeat. That's like receiving a slow IV drip of poison—remember the Room of Discouragement. It slows us down, it makes us doubt ourselves, and in far too many cases, it leads to us feeling stuck and paralyzed in our businesses. Sometimes for years on end. But we're going to bust you out.

Second Step—Time to Talk Back

The goal of this exercise isn't to create a 'burn list' of our worst thoughts about ourselves. The goal, which we aim for in the second and all important step, is to start talking back to this voice. Because when you think about it, what on earth right does your Inner Critic have, to be serving up distorted facts and half truths or worse, things that never have been and never will be true?

So our second step is to grab a colored pen—I often like to use a more optimistic color, like magenta or orange—and we are going to use the space you left between each limiting belief to talk back at, or even better, *sass back* your Inner Critic. For each limiting belief you want to think about the evidence of whether this statement is true or false, and what is really going on instead.

So, like me with my crazy post-massage hair, tempted to believe that *"everyone is looking at you and thinking you must be out of your mind"*, the counter thought that put my Inner Critic in its place was to realize, *"no, that isn't the case—it's Friday and I just went for a massage—I am living my best life!"*

Sometimes it can help to visualize this as a game of tennis where your Inner Critic serves a killer ball over the net right at you, and your job is to muster all of your strength and whack it back over the net as hard and fast as you can. We aren't going to let him or her have the last word, especially not when they are saying such crazy untrue things. And your Inner Critic really isn't that good at tennis. It's easier to win the point that you might think!

So, using our examples from before:

- *You have failed at everything you have ever done—this might become, "Actually I haven't failed at anything."*
- *You aren't good at making money— "Then how come I've made so much of it up to now?"*
- *You don't have a clue what you're doing— "That might have been true five years ago, but I've learned a ton since then."*
- *No one will buy this— "How do you know?? Can you predict the future?"*
- *You should have stayed in your corporate job— "I trusted my instincts and those instincts have brought me this far. They're not going to desert me now."*

You can get as creative as you like. There is no right or wrong, only what feels right or wrong to you. The goal of this exercise is to let out all of the pent up self-criticism and all the limiting beliefs you have been storing up, sometimes for months or even years, and finally allow the things that your Inner Critic loves to whisper to you to see the light of day.

Like the shapes in the dark of your childhood bedroom, there's nothing like shining a light on your limiting beliefs to help you realize that your Inner Critic is nothing but a harmless shadow from a pile of clothes.

And I can promise you, if you can do this even some of the time, you will see and feel the difference in your life and in your business. So many people the world over never have the breakthrough of realizing their Inner Critic is even there, let alone that what he or she is saying is not true. It is so easy to listen to our limiting beliefs on repeat and in doing so, sleepwalk through life—never feeling confident enough to reach out for the things that will bring us the fulfillment we crave in the world. And more than this, staying stuck in feeling like too much, instead of pursuing 'more'. Remember that your Inner Critic wants you to stay safe, but you won't necessarily *be* unsafe if you pursue peak fulfillment. And feeling fulfilled creates a level of safety that far outweighs the risk of the road to get there.

When Your Inner Critic Gets Sneaky

Now it could be that you are reading this and thinking, that's all fine when my limiting beliefs aren't true, Jessica, but what about when it's not so straightforward? What if your Inner Critic is telling you that you HAVE actually failed at everything you have tried before, and actually when you weigh it up it feels like they might be right?

We could counter this by listing out our achievements and the things we have done that haven't failed. But it's also helpful to understand that alongside limiting beliefs that are downright untrue, our Inner Critic can sometimes get a little clever and serve us up things that might 'technically' be true, or at least partially true. But as I say to my kids, *"if you have to use the word 'technically', that means it's not true enough"*. Maybe your Inner Critic is reminding you that you have made failed ventures in the past, and let's be real, if you're any kind of entrepreneur it is highly likely that you have experienced some degree of failure as you have grown and developed your business. I know I have! After all—failure is a central part of the entrepreneurial process.

It could be that this limiting belief comes from a situation that used to be true. Maybe you had a period of time where your business was extremely challenging, and all kinds of things failed. Maybe you went through a crisis period where sales slumped and revenue dropped, and you didn't know if you would make it through the other side. This has the double win for your Inner Critic of being something that *used to be true* as well as being something that you likely *feel shame about*, which makes it possible to be even more powerfully weaponized against you.

But the two things that your Inner Critic cannot withstand—visibility and scrutiny—are still just as effective here. *You HAVE actually failed at everything you have tried before,* says your Inner Critic. And it's just as important to talk back. Yes, maybe you have had failures in the past. Maybe you have been through times when it wasn't clear if your business would survive. But don't forget—your Inner Critic can't predict the future. We need to shine a light on the misbelief that it can, and that it has access to information that you don't. So, what can you tell yourself to counter this? Well, let's start with what has changed since you first experienced these things. What have you learned in the time since you failed at the thing you failed at? I often speak to women who are still feeling the sting of negative feedback from a corporate job they did a decade earlier. Or sometimes it's a failure from their childhood or teenage years that their Inner Critic is telling them is still relevant. This is why it's so powerful to remind yourself everything you've learned since this event. We progress and evolve so much even in a short space of time. I guarantee you, you have changed and grown since—but you may not have noticed yet. What resources can you draw on? We often have way more resilience and inner strength than we realize.

Your Inner Critic never gets to have the last word. *"Yes I have failed but I also learned and grew as a result"*.

And it might not feel like it, but failure is one of the strongest predictors of future success—if you learn from your mistakes and do it differently next time. Failure shows you have skin in the game, which is so much more valuable than just sitting on the sidelines. It's all forward progress.

The thing is, some of our limiting beliefs might be based on rational fears. Business failure is costly and devastating. It is reasonable to want to avoid this. But if we're honest, a lot of our fears are just low-quality fiction. And we already know that when trauma is present, we spend a lot of time reacting to things that aren't happening. The problem is our brains can't tell the difference between the things that are happening and the things that we fear might happen. Which makes it even more important that we don't let our Inner Critic jump in and convince us that we are on the wrong path and about to make a terrible mistake.

When Your Inner Critic Is Your Traumatized Inner Child

I want to make a comment here for anyone who experienced trauma in their childhood or their early adult life and who recognizes that when their Inner Critic speaks, it is actually showing up as their traumatized Inner Child or their traumatized younger self.

It is still perfectly valid to undertake this 'talking back' exercise but we can practice it with less sass and more compassion. We don't need to be cruel to our Inner Child—she already went through a lot. In this circumstance I take a slightly different approach. When our traumatized Inner Child or Inner Teenager shows up as our Inner Critic it will say things like, *"This isn't safe for you because remember X event or experience."* Therefore, it says, *"Never do this again because A+B=C and that will always be the outcome"*.

Your Inner Child is often scared after experiencing harm, and she is right to be. This isn't irrational—harm already happened. A powerful way to counter this is to gently say to your Inner Child, *"I know that X happened. And it shouldn't have happened, and I am sorry you experienced that. You are safe now. We don't need to be afraid because I am an adult now and I can keep you safe."* And sometimes it really helps to wrap your arms across your body and give yourself a 'self hug.' And we can turn this into an embodiment—not just hearing the words but allowing them to absorb into your body and soothe the difficult emotions that are coming up. *You are safe. You are loved. You don't need to be afraid of this happening*. But—if this is a delicate area for you because of past trauma, always get the support of a trained trauma therapist who can help you process the trauma safely. Sometimes therapies such as EMDR (Eye Movement Desensitization and Reprocessing) can be a really effective way of turning the volume down on your trauma or a more effective way of addressing the distress of your Inner Child.

The truth is that the Inner Critic gets loud when we do expansive growth work, so if you follow the step of *Connecting to Abundance* in the last chapter you should *expect* your Inner Critic to show up and to sound urgent. Your Inner Critic is trying to stop you from making this journey. They want you to stay safe. But it's not rational. Remember, they have no additional knowledge. Everything your subconscious mind serves up is based on a past trauma (even if it was Little-t) experienced by a younger version of you or something they have no actual knowledge of. It may even be based on generational trauma—things that did not happen to you but that happened to your predecessors or ancestors.

It is essential that we understand this so that when it happens, we understand correctly what it means. It doesn't mean you are wrong to go on the journey of looking for your 'more'. It doesn't mean that you have overestimated your gifts. It doesn't mean you would be better to resign yourself to feeling like too much for the rest of your life. More than anything, your Inner Critic loves to make you feel the stigma of being too much and like you are beyond help. But only you can decide if that is actually true for you! Remember—if your Inner Critic is activated, it means that you're doing something right because it means that you are on the road to discovering your 'more' and realizing your peak fulfillment.

Building the Muscle of Talking Back

So, what is the result over time of practicing this 'talking back' exercise to our Inner Critic, and hitting back the limiting beliefs they insist on serving you like tennis balls firing at you across the net?

What you will find as you do this 'talking back' exercise is that it becomes easier to not believe the things your Inner Critic is telling you.

It becomes easier to remove the day-to-day mindset blocks in your path.

When we turn this into a regular practice, we stop procrastinating and resisting the things that, deep down, we know will take us exactly where we want to go. We stop abandoning our big vision and settling for something smaller. We don't fall into mindset whiplash and abruptly flee. We don't take up residence in the Room of Discouragement. Instead we gain the ability to see through the lies of our Inner Critic and by connecting with our Higher Self, we rise above the depths the Inner Critic is trying to take us to. Your Higher Self is always there to send you a rope ladder to escape. (And this is why connecting to abundance is such a valuable step to know how to take!)

It is the most magical feeling when you realize that you are making progress in this area and finding yourself able to self-correct and follow through with the aligned actions you want to be taking. We all still have these doubts sometimes, but when you discover how to switch off the radio station of negativity your Inner Critic wants to broadcast, it makes the journey of looking for your 'more' feel lighter and easier. This is what helps us to realize that being too much is the greatest gift we could ask for. We can finally see the ways we feel like just the right amount, and even that we are enjoying the journey, at last.

Now that we've explored how to talk back to the Inner Critic, we are ready to create some Seven Figure Aligned Actions. And this is exactly what we are going to be focusing on in Chapter 8.

CHAPTER SUMMARY

- The Secret Your Inner Critic Doesn't Want You to Know
- Turning Down the Volume
- First Step—Let Your Inner Critic Speak
- Second Step—Time to Talk Back
- When Your Inner Critic Gets Sneaky
- When Your Inner Critic Is Your Traumatized Inner Child
- Building the Muscle of Talking Back

8 Feeling for Seven Figure Aligned Actions

We have started to lay out the framework of how we transition from knowing we are too much (and feeling good about it!) in Part 1, to how to go on the journey to look for your 'more' in Chapters 6 and 7. We have looked at Connecting to Abundance, and then Dealing with the Inner Critic so we don't get derailed or experience the dreaded 'mindset whiplash' that either makes us flee or causes us to get stuck in the Room of Discouragement.

So now you have started to connect with your Higher Self, opened the channel of your intuition and swept away the protests of your Inner Critic, you are ready to start feeling for the true building blocks of Radical Self Improvement and your path to peak fulfillment. You are ready for the third step of our *Connecting, Dealing and Feeling* framework, to start identifying your Seven Figure Aligned Actions—the 'doing' part of the process! Take note here because we are finally ready for the 'how'.

But what is an aligned action? Let's unpack this and learn how you can start taking powerful action to bring your seven figure vision into fruition. This is where things get really exciting!

The Two Things Aligned Actions Are Not

You might feel like you know where you are with the concept of 'actions', especially coming from a corporate background where everything that needs doing after a meeting is assigned to a particular person. I've also noticed that when I introduce my clients to aligned actions, they will often say, "*Oh, of course, my aligned actions are just my To Do List.*"

So here's something we need to get really clear about. Aligned actions are neither 'meeting actions', nor your to do list. It makes perfect sense why you might assume that aligned actions are the actions that follow from a coaching call that sort of fits in the same category of a corporate meeting. Because let's face it—as an entrepreneur, especially if you're still a solopreneur, you might be used to picking up ALL of the actions in your team meetings (especially if it's just you in the team!). And it might be your continual experience as a business owner that you run with a consistently long and convoluted to do list—the kind that can feel like the bane of your existence! It's always overflowing, it never gets fully completed and it dominates your working week. It's actually your inner Drill Sergeant in the form of a list. And it makes you feel pretty lousy.

But this is another Value Over Volume moment. Remember how we talked about growing your consulting business through value not volume back in Chapter 6? A small number of high-paying clients instead of a vast number of low-paying clients.

Aligned actions work exactly the same. You are not going to be working 15 hour days, cranking out a huge *volume* of actions. We get to seven figures by feeling for the most aligned, strategic, meaningful actions, and starting with these first. It can—and often does—mean that you get to your goal on a far quicker and easier path, and this is what makes it such an essential filter to apply.

In fact, this may come as a shock—but as the CEO of a consulting company that is on its way to having a seven figure turnover, your days of having a to do list are over. Does that feel a little traumatic to comprehend?? Even if it does right now, I promise you, it is the most powerful way to break the connection between you doing things and progress happening in your business. Breaking up with your to do list is an important step that creates the transition from being a six figure solopreneur who does all the things with no help, to a seven figure CEO who leverages a team to get things done without having to do them personally. It's separating out *You the Person*, and *You the Business*, and it's an essential part of the process of growing from six to seven figures.

Most six figure solopreneur consultants will default to a volume-based business model, where growth is achieved by adding a greater *volume* of clients. But we need to stop trying to grow your consulting business by adding more—more low-priced clients, more delivery team members, more leads, more sales, more small cogs—and instead transition to that wondrous thing—a *value*-based business model.

When we try to get to seven figures by doing more of the things that got you to six figures, you get tired and burned out, you have to work harder, there is more chaos and friction, and you end up needing a huge (and expensive) team of people to make it happen. The business revenue does increase on a volume-based model, but because you need more people to make it happen, so does the cost of running the business. In fact, you can actually make less profit even though the business revenue has gone up. Technically the business has grown, but you are not better off as a result. Sounds crazy right??

But when you can grow your consulting business with a *value-based* business model, you are essentially growing the business first and foremost by aiming for the top of the market instead of the lowest common denominator/race to the bottom, where you win work by being the cheapest. And by implementing a value-based model, you can increase revenue AND profits with fewer clients. When you can do the bulk of your work as an expert advisor to your clients instead of working as a 'done-for-you' freelance consultant who needs to bill by the hour and work a ton of hours to increase revenue, you free up your time exponentially. This is one of the central themes in my work with my clients. I call it Working Less and Earning More, and it's a game-changer.

We want to break the correlation of hours worked and money earned. Your clients are not paying you for the hours, they are paying you for the years of experience you have gained in your corporate career. If you are a thought leader and an expert in your field, they are paying you for the years. And this is why you need to grow past running your business from your to do list. And it is also why an aligned action is not 'actions from a meeting' or a to do list. It's not about the volume of tasks you're doing, it's about identifying the tasks that make the biggest impact in achieving your goal and ONLY doing those things.

Can you see how much your to do list is a symbol for playing small in your business? It's time to break free. We are busting you out of six figure solopreneurism, the wearing of many hats in the business, constantly feeling frazzled and fearing burnout is just around the corner. We are busting you out of feeling like too much and not enough at the same time. It's time to start showing up as the CEO.

And guess what? Seven Figure Aligned Actions are the key to this transformation.

The Magic of Seven Figure Aligned Actions

So, if an aligned action is not a to do list, what actually is it? An aligned action is a next step that gets delivered as a spark of inspiration. It is something that draws you in, even if it feels insane and slightly scary. Aligned actions aren't the things that are put on the back burner or get done *'if I have time'*. An aligned action requires action right now, today, within 24 hours, this week. And this is a really important part because I know that, if you're reading this, you probably have a very disciplined sense of duty in your work, and you have spent years gritting your teeth and doing things at work that you don't really want to be doing, but feel you need to for the sake of the client. And even learning how to talk with enthusiasm in your corporate career about things that you don't feel any genuine excitement about.

Remember the Dissociated Self, who has switched off her emotions and authentic self so she can get through the day? This is the opposite. An aligned action makes your heart sing. It feels exciting, full of possibility. It is in the category of *"Well, now I've had this thought I can't NOT do this"*. That is the magic of alignment—the feeling that this action is important, it has meaning.

We get so used to doing things that feel meaning*less*, especially in a corporate workplace. Writing reports that no one will ever read. Showing up to meetings where nothing gets agreed and nothing moves forward. Having 'productive conversations' where nothing gets said or heard. When an action is aligned for you, it is like a magical rope ladder that takes you up and off the conventional path of your Dissociated Self and puts you on the path of your most actualized self, your Higher Self, your Seven Figure Self. And in doing so, you avoid the chutes the Inner Critic laid for you to fall down. This is why your Higher Self is so important.

Ultimately, what is the difference between your Dissociated Self and your Higher Self? Your Higher Self takes the action and does the things that elevate you off the path of un-fulfillment. Your Higher Self elevates you beyond the Evil Twin version of too much. Your Higher Self draws you off the conventional path by sending you aligned actions through the medium of your intuition, like a trail of breadcrumbs in the woods or stepping stones that appear one at a time to help you across the lake.

Connecting to Your Higher Self

What does it mean to receive messages from your intuition? If that's an inbox, how do we check it? This is why our first step of Connecting to Abundance is so important. When you are more dialed into your Higher Self, your Seven Figure Self, than you are to your Dissociated Self or your Inner Critic, you will find yourself having little sparks of inspiration. This happens all through the day and in all kinds of low-key decisions from what to eat for breakfast through to what time to go to bed at night. And you may have heard people talk about triggers, but have you heard of glimmers? These are the small moments of joy and fulfilment that are easily missed but once you know to look for them—we see them everywhere. Ever wonder why we all love the sight of a rainbow? Or a butterfly? Or a hummingbird? We are wired to see glimmers but so often we blink and miss them. Imagine how it must feel for your Seven Figure Self who sends glimmers every day, only to have us be so busy with our fears and our to do list that we don't even notice them!

And this is the important part—when you are in your Dissociated Self, who cannot feel her body or her emotions and is just going through the motions doing the things she feels resigned to, or the things that are expected of her, it is like logging out of the channel of your intuition. Every impulse you have to do something different gets ignored. You are stuck in low fulfillment. Conversely, when you start to listen to your body, feel your emotions, keep an open channel with your Higher Self, and notice these little messages, everything starts to shift.

It might feel strange to think about keeping an open channel with your Higher Self. Does that mean sit and meditate in a circle of lit candles? I guess it could! But ultimately, it is about seeking the wisdom of your Higher Self and exploring in any given situation what her perspective would be. How would she advise you? Remember my question to myself—*"What does abundance look like in this situation?"* It is about opening up your awareness and getting curious. It's about letting go of the need to blindly accept your body's knee-jerk reaction, especially if you have been in your Dissociated Self for a long period. And this is where we start to realize that your too-much-ness has been sending you the message, possibly for decades, that you need to look for more. That where you are is not what you are meant for—and that your Higher Self knows the path to follow in order to get to your 'more'.

How to Listen

Here are some questions to ask yourself that will open up your awareness. *What is my first instinct? Who was speaking when that thought came up? What does my Higher Self think instead? What intuitive sparks are coming through?*

Let's illustrate this with an example. Remember my client Rosalyn from Chapter 3, who had a successful consulting business? She kept receiving an internal prompt, *"What if I started a group for women?"* She wanted to create something to support executive women to build their influence and impact. I have spoken to all kinds of women who have a vision like this. I encourage them to ask those questions to open up their awareness. What's striking to watch is the very moment they overcome their first instinct, the knee-jerk reaction to resist the idea, when they stop batting away the inspiration and instead start to entertain the idea and allow it to expand.

It's the moment that we shift from *"I can't do that. That's ridiculous!"* to *"What if I could...?"* Fixed negative thinking shifts to curiosity. And from a place of *"What if I could?"*, this is a perfect moment to consult your Higher Self. What does she think? Does this feel aligned? Do you feel that intuitive "yes" reverberating through your whole body? Does it feel exciting? Does it feel expansive?

It's ok if it feels scary or even a bit terrifying. Going outside of your comfort zone will always feel this way. If you are shifting from the conventional path to the highway of your Higher Self, you are going against your internal programming which will always want to keep everything small and safe. Your subconscious mind has a strong pull to stop you from switching paths—even though it's so much better for you to be on the path to high fulfillment than staying stuck in low fulfilment. That's how we know your subconscious mind doesn't have all the answers. And it is all too ready to trigger the mindset whiplash that will send you straight home. But now you know how to deal with the Inner Critic, and once you've done that, you'll find that this journey is made up of small, manageable steps. All you have to do is feel for the abundance energy and follow the breadcrumbs.

You don't have to blindly throw yourself at a brick wall—you know when we almost take the approach of doing the opposite of what we would do normally but not in a thought-through way, more like blindly flipping your instinct to its opposite without any connection to the action itself. This might create contrast but it isn't alignment—because we are still failing to hear our intuition despite the bold actions we might be taking. This is why it is so important to Connect to Abundance and listen for your intuitive voice—so that you can feel for the alignment that will guide your next steps.

Feeling for Your Seven Figure Aligned Action

So, let's continue this example of Rosalyn and her big idea, so we can really get some clarity around what it looks like to find an aligned action.

I will always ask clients this question when we are talking about ways they want to elevate or new things they want to grow towards. While you are still in the energy of your Higher Self, the version of you who truly believes that this is possible, what intuitively feels like the next step to take?

This won't be a giant leap where you burn down your existing business, rebrand for the new venture, fire all your clients. It can be exhilarating to imagine this sometimes—especially when you have been dutifully dissociated in your business for some time, but aligned actions don't always need to be big and dramatic. Instead, what is the next aligned step towards the vision that you have?

It is usually something incredibly simple but with very high impact. A straightforward action that will powerfully move the needle. We want your business to become something that feels easy to run and that creates revenue effortlessly. So, the aligned action will often be something that reflects this. *Call X person. Book a venue. Tell a legacy client we aren't going to renew their contract.*

It's not always important what it is *specifically*, the thing that really matters is what pattern are you breaking, and what new pattern are you setting up instead? Because when you start to show up differently, and act differently, especially when you have been stuck in your Dissociated Self for a long time, things start to shift. Remember our pattern from Chapter 4—Think the belief, Say the belief, Act out the belief, Receive the belief.

In Rosalyn's case, her first aligned action was to create space with her existing clients. She had been drawn into a pattern of meetings all day, every day, and this meant she had no space to do anything else but be available for her clients. So, she renegotiated her existing contracts and carved out a couple of days in the week where she wasn't available for calls. Her next aligned action was to reach out to some of the women she had in mind for the program and invite them in. Both felt challenging, but the second was decidedly scarier!

'How' Is a Shrinking Word

Now I know if you're reading this there's a chance you are absolutely great at planning. In detail. It is a skill that many of us, as high-achieving women have in spades. It is probably one of the reasons you got insanely good results in your corporate career. I have found that a lot of my clients excel at this because it also provides a very effective way to deal with anxiety or trauma. If we plan everything to the letter, we feel like we're in control.

I know because I used to do this, too. When you feel out of control as a child because the adults around you can't handle their emotions, it makes perfect sense that you would become a world expert at managing uncertain situations for yourself and other people with planning, spreadsheets, Post-Its, color-coding, the whole shebang. The other word for this is *hypervigilance*—I think of hypervigilance as trying to be the captain in control of the ship, manning all of the computer screens at the same time. We often have a (crazy) belief—*"If I can just keep everything in sight, nothing bad will happen."*

Now there's a few reasons that this is not a good place to be. First of all, hypervigilance leads to heightened anxiety which no one enjoys. I had incredibly high anxiety when my first son was a newborn, that meant I was afraid to fall asleep in case something bad happened to him and I wasn't awake to stop it. It was of no value to either of us that I couldn't fall asleep, because, second of all, the belief we can prevent all bad things from happening is a total fallacy. Of course you can't control everything, even if you are internally manning all the computer screens. Oh, the number of times I have had this conversation with myself! There is actually very little we can control, and it might feel reassuring to believe that we are making a difference through our hypervigilance, but in reality, we are just exhausting ourselves trying to keep too many balls in the air and do what is not possible for a human to do. Not to mention, when we do this for the benefit of other people, we are robbing them of the opportunity to take responsibility for their own situation and emotions.

But the main reason that planning out every detail of every minute of every day in your consulting business isn't a good idea, is that it leads to us making everything way too small. The way to make this journey to your 'more', isn't to have a minute-by-minute plan, where you decide how everything will play out and what you will do at every turn in advance. I often say to clients—*"How is a shrinking word"*. And it might sound crazy if you're a serial planner, but we actually don't need to know the full picture of how we will achieve something. What we need is self-trust—the knowledge that we can trust ourselves to follow the path in real-time as it appears.

I have had clients who made micro-plans for their every move in business for the year ahead, and guess what the result is. You run the plan and either it doesn't work out the way you thought, leading to mindset whiplash and the Room of Discouragement. Or—you run the plan and it goes exactly as you thought, and you do everything you said you would but guess what. It doesn't feel exciting or expansive. It feels boring as hell! Because you did a great job executing a business plan that you can now see should have been much, much bigger. It made sense in the moment that you made it at the start of the year—but you didn't account for the growth you would experience as the year went on. The exciting thing about going on the journey to your 'more,' is that there is the possibility of growth AT EVERY STAGE OF THE JOURNEY.

So, what you actually want to do—no surprises here—is *Connect, Deal and Feel.* Connect to Abundance, Deal with the Inner Critic, Feel for the Seven Figure Aligned Action, and execute it. Then—you connect to abundance again and begin the process over. When clients commit to this, I have seen them make compound, quantum growth in their business as the year goes on as they are able to hold and execute a bigger and bigger version of the 'more' they are seeking. This is why alongside your massive to do list, we are going to bless and release your minute-by-minute plan for your consulting business this year, and maybe even put it in the garbage. With love. Instead we are going to identify the next Seven Figure Aligned Actions.

What if I Can't Feel My Intuition?

So it might be that you're reading this and thinking, *Jessica, this is great but seriously. I feel nothing from my intuition. I'm not even sure I have an intuitive voice. There is nothing there to hear.*

First of all, I want to say, don't weigh yourself down with trying to do it right or find the right answer. And I know that can be super hard and frustrating for my ex-corporate high-achievers! When it comes to intuition, there is no right answer—all we have is 'in alignment' or 'out of alignment,' and this isn't fixed. This is why it is so important for us to be able to be present and in the moment because we need to be able to understand what our intuition is calling us to today.

Another question I often get asked is *"How can I tell if this is out of alignment or I'm just in resistance?"* If you find that you don't want to do something in your business like host an event or launch a new service that you were previously excited about—what does this mean? And the quick answer is—your body knows the difference. If you keep leaning into the step you're thinking about taking—and the big, abundant goal sitting behind it—and really pay attention to what body sensations are coming up or what thoughts you're having, you will discover the answer.

But back to the issue of what you can do if you feel nothing from your intuitive voice, the question I would want to ask is *"What are you avoiding?"* If you are a planner and love to be in control, it can be really destabilizing to listen to your intuitive voice. Sometimes we are just getting to a place where it feels like all our ducks are lined up in business and you suddenly realize, *no, this isn't the path. This was in alignment before, but something has shifted, and I've grown past it.* It can be inconvenient to say the least—and costly, not to mention annoying!

Even though our intuition alone can lead us away from things we are sure were in alignment for us, it is always worth taking a beat to reflect. Get quiet and think about what might be going on for you internally. Journalling can be really helpful to get clarity about this. What are you feeling? I can promise you—you are never feeling nothing! What emotions are present? Is there something uncomfortable or inconvenient coming up for you?

I have clients who find this easy and others who are effectively learning to speak the language of their body and emotions for the first time. I have actually noticed that, typically, the women I meet fall into two broad categories linked to family origins. I am convinced that it is to do with the kind of child or sibling you were required to be.

For the women who learned to be the 'good girl,' the dutiful one who managed everyone in the family's mess and set her own needs to one side, this can be extremely difficult. You cannot easily discern what your body needs, what you truly want or hear your intuitive voice because your entire life's training has been about squashing those instincts down and doing and being what other people require of you.

Conversely, if you were more of the 'attention seeker' in the family who craved being seen and heard, whose emotions burst out of you and couldn't be contained, it isn't as difficult to discern your inner voice or your intuition. I tend to find that for women in this situation you have been waiting your whole life for someone to ask you how you feel about anything and everything! But the challenge for you is to not just hear your intuition and dismiss it or bat it away as you probably have done many times before, but to learn how to *act* on it.

Building the Muscle of Self Trust

Learning to trust your intuition is something that gets easier with practice. Just like developing a growth mindset, it is a muscle we need to build up. When I first started my coaching business, I found it excruciating to trust my intuition. I have had roles in the past where I was actively discouraged from using my initiative and you may have had the same experience. The boss who wants to check all your emails before you send them. Who always disagrees with your decisions. Who will always make an arbitrary correction just to make a point. I came into my business with a strong distrust of my intuition and the strong belief that I see in a lot of women I speak to that *"I don't know what to do."* And because we don't trust ourselves, we want people to rescue us at every turn. I have had times when I needed to make decisions in my business about what to say yes or no to and I was shocked to realize I missed the days of having a boss who could make all those decisions for me!

But I have to say—sometimes asking other people for advice is the worst thing you can do. I see this a lot for women entrepreneurs, and I have also done it myself—we feel overwhelmed because we don't know what to do. Instead of sitting with this discomfort and feeling into what the resonant decision and aligned action is, we ask someone else what they think. We then ask someone else's opinion too, to balance it out. We keep asking more and more people what they think we should do, and at no stage do we feel any calmer or any closer to an answer. I have occasionally had clients who engage another coach while we are working together and unless this is managed helpfully, it can become a crazy tennis match of opinions in all directions —or as we used to say in my London career, a bun fight!—and no action taken at all. I have clients who sometimes want me to prescribe exactly what they should do, but often it's much more valuable to help them access their intuition. I have to say though, they don't always love having their coach answer a question with a question!

I'm not saying never ask for advice, but I will say—know exactly why you need the advice from that person. Ask yourself, am I going to ask them because I don't have enough subject matter expertise, or because I don't trust myself to make this decision right now? If it's the latter, I guarantee you, you can get all the advice in the world, and you still won't know what to do. Build the muscle of self trust and you'll always be able to access the insight you need.

Pay Attention to Your First Instinct

How can we break this cycle of overwhelm and feeling like we don't know what to do? It can actually be very simple. The next time you are at a crossroads in your business, from *"Should I speak at this conference?"* to *"Should I hire out this position and if so, who should I hire?"*—pay attention to your first instinct. I have struggled so much to learn to trust my intuition. And I noticed I was often falling into a pattern where I would think of the thing I wanted to do, but then I would second-guess myself and add in a ton of other options and then end up full of anxiety and totally frozen. It would happen with the big things but also with the small things.

A few months ago I was staying in a hotel, traveling for business, and had a couple of hours to kill. Inspiration hit! I would go to the hotel gym. But then the pattern started: *I haven't got the right shirt with me. I don't know where the gym is. They might have the wrong sort of machines.* Isn't it amazing what our brains conjure up to throw us into a loop! After a few moments of these thoughts, I could feel myself disappearing into overwhelm. When this happens, you have to catch the thought that you don't know what to do, stop it in its tracks and pay attention to your first instinct. For me in that moment, I knew what I needed to do. I got up just as I was and found the gym and did my workout.

It can be this simple to find your aligned action when you are feeling in a fog of overwhelm and indecision. You will likely find yourself going out of your comfort zone more and more as time goes on, doing things you maybe have never done and going to places you might not have been before. This might be literally going to geographic places you have never been, but also figuratively, taking your consulting business to heights you have never seen. And here's the thing.

Just do it. Seriously.

When we delay and delay, we are selling ourselves out and staying stuck when we don't actually need to stay stuck. Why take the long road when you can take the direct path and have the thing you actually want? Yes, this is a path that requires courage. But everything you want is on the other side. And when you can live out the 3 steps of Connecting to Abundance, Dealing with the Inner Critic and Feeling for Seven Figure Aligned Actions, you are equipped for the journey in a way you have never been before.

Follow your energy. Follow the path to 'more' because then you won't feel like too much any more. You will feel like the exact right amount. And in Part Three, the final part of this book, we're going to dial up the real talk so you know exactly what to expect on this ride of a lifetime.

CHAPTER SUMMARY

- The Two Things Aligned Actions Are Not
- The Magic of Seven Figure Aligned Actions
- Connecting to Your Higher Self
- How to Listen
- Feeling for Your Seven Figure Aligned Action
- 'How' Is a Shrinking Word
- What if I Can't Feel My Intuition?
- Building the Muscle of Self Trust
- Pay Attention to Your First Instinct

PART THREE

Letting Go of Hard, Letting It Be Easy

Welcome to Part Three of our journey together! So far, we have taken a tour through what it means to be too much (and proud of it!), how to start your journey to your 'more', and the steps you need to follow on the journey of *Connecting, Dealing and Feeling*—Connecting to Abundance, Dealing with the Inner Critic, and Feeling for the Seven Figure Aligned Actions that will connect you to your path of peak fulfillment. And once you've found this path, you will start to notice that your too much starts to feel like just the right amount.

Now, a lot of business books would have finished at the end of Chapter 8. *You've caught the vision, you've learned the framework, and now you're on your own. Go figure it all out!*

But this has never felt right to me, and I don't think this is the right approach. In my own personal journey of 10 years as an entrepreneur and in the work I do with my clients, it's all well and good to know the theory but the moment you need the most support and encouragement is when the plane is in the air and you're actually doing it. Because it's when you set out on the journey that the work really begins and shit gets real. It doesn't matter if you know exactly where you want to aim for, and your bag is all packed and ready to go. Until the plane lands, it's all still theoretical.

Now I'd like to state something here and I hope that you won't think it's big-headed of me. But one of the things I do best as a coach, and I think my clients would back me up on this, is real talk. I don't make it sound easy when it's hard, and I don't airbrush out all of the messy parts. I don't require you to pretend that bits of the journey aren't difficult or frustrating. I'm not an Insta-perfect kind of person, and I don't expect you to be either. Unless you're into that. (In which case, I would probably still encourage you to embrace your authentic self but, you know, in a supportive kind of way. LOL)

So, this final part is all about what really happens when you are in the weeds, doing the work, Connecting to Abundance, getting hit with your Inner Critic, Feeling for the Seven Figure Aligned Actions, and wondering what on earth is going on. And straightaway, maybe this book would sell more copies if I made it sound super easy and airbrushed out all the mess from the journey. But there are plenty of books out there already that play this game, and honestly? I think we all know that the journey can get hella messy. So I'm going to opt for truth telling instead.

I actually think that Part Three amounts to the most important leg of the journey we're on together, from feeling like too much to finding your 'more'. We're going to cover some important ground together so that as you start to step into this phase of your journey you know that I've got your back, 100%.

So, in the spirit of real talk, I'm going to be introducing you to a pivotal concept in Part Three and this is:

Letting go of hard, and letting it be easy.

Sounds straightforward, doesn't it? But I have to tell you, we can be so invested in making business hard. So often, we have the total expectation that life and business will be hard. As we have already covered in Chapter 5, most of us have been raised on scarcity, and then we have this scarcity belief reinforced constantly by the news, social media, people around us, our culture. And we welcome it. We love to default to struggle. We tell ourselves that business success is hard won, involving copious amounts of our blood, sweat, and tears. We shun advice that requires us to involve other people, believing instead we have to be self-sufficient and super strong. It can feel like the rules of business dictate we have to do everything the hard way.

We cannot get help because that is 'cheating', somehow. Getting help or enjoying the journey means taking a shortcut, when we can only win the game of business if we do everything by every stone-cold letter of the rules.

And this is another one of those *'if you say so'* moments that you might remember from Chapter 4.

Does growing your business to seven figures have to be hard? *If you say so.*

There is also the option to allow it to be easy. So, in this final part, I am going to show you how to choose easy as you look for your 'more' and find fulfillment in growing your consulting business to seven figures.

This is something I have had to learn! As I've already shared, I love to make things complicated and hard, adding layers and layers in my quest to optimize and be the best I can be. That's great and all, but that is not the game of business, my friend. We may be wired for Radical Self Improvement but, remember, we also need its magical cousin, Radical Self Acceptance. Instead, we are going to follow the pattern of our blueprint from Part Two, *Connecting, Dealing and Feeling*. The theory is great, but the practice is so much more rewarding, and I'm not going to leave you hanging.

So then, in Part Three, we are going to look at why it is hard to look for your 'more' and grow a seven figure consulting business, and how to make it easy. We're going to look at what I call the Big Excuses Playbook—some of the stories we tell ourselves on the journey when we're tempted to quit and throw in the towel. Finally, we're going to pull it all together and discover how you can build a life and business that makes your too much feel like just the right amount.

Ready to let go of hard and instead let it be easy? Me too—let's do this!

9 Why It's Hard

Why is the journey of business growth so simple and yet at the same time, it feels so hard?

We have already talked about the concept of 'mindset whiplash'—when we are going strong and going big and feeling so good about the things we are about to achieve, only to experience a roadblock that makes it feel like our courage and confidence have totally deserted us. Our expansiveness evaporates, leaving behind only fear and even horror. We cannot believe we were so stupid to think we could do something so big. Our Inner Critic has grabbed the wheel and does everything they can do to get us to make a U-turn and head back home to safety.

In its simplest form, this dramatic experience is captured in a single word—'resistance'. And it is essential that we understand resistance, so that when it crops up—and I guarantee you that it will before too long—you can recognize it and know what it is and what it isn't.

Misreading the Road in Front of Us

We think we know what's in front of us when mindset whiplash kicks in. But it's a knee-jerk reaction prompted by fear. Out of nowhere, it feels like we've made a terrible mistake in setting out on the journey to 'more'. It feels like the only option is to flee home. Expansive business growth means extending past what has previously felt achievable. It can often feel deeply *un*comfortable because we are leaving the familiarity of the thing that feels infinitely comfortable—the comfort zone! We're not driving down the same streets we've known for years, we're in new territory. And just like that moment where you drive your rental car out of an unfamiliar foreign airport, it can feel like everything looks totally different and you have no idea where to go. Entrepreneurship can be *really* overwhelming because as your business grows, everything looks different. And you're suddenly making all kinds of decisions all day every day that you have no idea how to make. So it totally follows that when we're on the road to 'more', we can feel overwhelmed by the unfamiliarity of our surroundings and how different life and business suddenly feel. Neurologists have discovered that when we're under stress, the pre-frontal cortex of the brain shuts down, which leaves us less able to think rationally and far more likely to react with heightened emotions. And so it figures that when mindset whiplash kicks in all we want to do is flee. But what we're missing is that mindset whiplash isn't a dead end—it's a crossroads.

What do I mean by this? I want to take you back a step for a moment, to the second you felt that jolt moment. Maybe you didn't expect your Inner Critic to dig in hard at the first sign of trouble. That's what the Inner Critic thinks their job is. The problem is, you didn't know to expect them to do it. What this looks like is you feel your confidence crumbling. And then you feel that your only option is to label everything you just committed to as a huge mistake.

What do we do when we have made a mistake? We grab the eraser and rub it all out. *No,* you mutter to yourself as you rub, *I shouldn't have listened to my Higher Self. I shouldn't have believed that I could do something bigger. There is no 'more' for me. I just need to make my peace with being too much and get used to having to make myself smaller for other people.*

I am willing to bet that as a person who feels like too much, you have experienced this many times. But—it wasn't a dead end where the only option is to retreat back home. You reached a crossroads, which means *you are at choice.* You get to make decisions. You can decide to abandon ship and flee back home. Or—you can do the work of addressing the protests of your Inner Critic and make a balanced decision about whether you want to retreat and flee from your journey to 'more', or whether you want to beat a new path forward.

If you can read the road correctly and see the crossroads instead of just making that handbrake turn and fleeing back, you have a skill that a majority of the world's population has no awareness of. And it's an absolute superpower that will serve you time and again on your journey to 'more'.

So why does this happen more when we are new to the journey? I'm glad you asked, because I have a rather gross story to share about this.

A Lifetime of Gunk

When I was a first-time mom with a baby at home, we used to sit him in a little bath seat during bath time. It kept his head out of the water and the sucky pads on the bottom of it meant he couldn't slip and slide around too much (because is it me? Babies and toddlers become like slippery eels when wet and soapy!). But one evening during bath time, I noticed a small black flake in the bath. And then another. I popped my son out of the bath for a moment and picked up the bath seat. I turned it over and saw the entire underneath and insides of the seat were covered in disgusting, gunky black mold. I know right? Screaming face emoji.

Ready for the parallel? Because this is what it's like when it comes to the mindset work required when you are starting your journey to 'more'. You may have spent your entire life listening to your Inner Critic and believing everything they say to you, without ever questioning whether what they say is true or fair. Because, up to this point, like me with the baby bath seat, you haven't realized that the gunk is even there. So, at the point that you start to shine a light around the place, it feels like it is everywhere because it has been building up and building up your whole life. And here's the thing. That night, I gave the bath seat an epic level clean. Bleach, scrubbing out every last nook and cranny. And seriously, the amount of gunk that came out. Even nine years on, it still makes me shudder! Such a rookie mom! *Oh wait, I'm supposed to clean the underneath of the bath seat?! No one ever told me that!*

As we saw in Chapters 6 and 7, if you're like most people you probably won't have even realized there IS a voice speaking when you receive limiting beliefs, or feel that sinking feeling when it starts to tell you you're doing it all wrong. You will just receive your negative thoughts as literal truth. *"This is just how the world is. It's a hostile place. You are a small and insignificant person among billions. Life is hard. Money is scarce. You're not that special."* Our Inner Critic loves to whisper these things and many others to us all day every day. This is a normal part of the human experience. And every poisonous thought that your brain has served you up for, honestly, decades of your life, is like the black mold that has been festering undisturbed.

But my experience of turning over that bath seat is what it's like when you realize that your mindset has been sludgy gunk your whole life. At first, it can feel like all you do is journal: you talk back to the limiting beliefs, and you feel the complaints and accusations of your Inner Critic rising to fever pitch. You question again whether this journey to your 'more' is all a huge mistake. It can feel like it takes AGES to get back to zero.

But, just like me scrubbing out the gunk on the bath seat, you will get to a place where the Inner Critic doesn't derail you in the same way. Where you can recognize their voice instantly and know on instinct that it might be compelling, but it isn't the truth. The gunk might still build up sometimes, but you know how to deal with it now. All it needs is a quick wipe around. You'll never have to tackle a lifetime's worth of gunk again.

You can go back to Chapter 7 of this book any time you need to for a quick refresher. But you can also:

Create a simple daily mindset practice. Instead of just documenting the struggles on the journey, I love to journal on all the signs of progress I can see and train my brain to see abundance instead of scarcity. You need a daily dose of abundance and this is a great way to give it to yourself.

Take every thought captive. Notice the moments in your day where you fall into scarcity or discouragement. Remind yourself that you are gloriously free to think something better.

Work with a coach like me. We are great at helping you see the mindset blocks you might not even realize you have, because none of us can read the label from inside the jar.

Tag in your entrepreneur friends to the conversation. It's amazing how much we can't see our own BS at times, but our friends can (if they are tapped into abundance too!)

Be part of a high-level business community like my group container for women, the Seven Figures Club. One of the things I love about my Seven Figures Club ladies is the way they hold space for one another and call out each other's Inner Critics. They often hear the feedback from one another more readily than when I've said it. When that happens, I sit back in my chair, take a sip of coffee and watch the breakthroughs happen—it's all good growth and I'm here for it!

As we saw in Chapter 4, we believe 100% of the things we say to ourselves—even more so when there is trauma in your backstory—so it is always important to make sure we are saying things that are actually true. In my experience of working with women consultants and running my own business for the last 10 years, we are so often convinced that we are failing when everyone else around us sees a totally different picture.

We can be so fearful that in believing the signs of progress in our businesses, we are believing things that are untrue—choosing hopeless optimism or delusion instead of the hard facts of the situation. But honestly, when I started to work on this in my own business, I realized that for my entire life I had believed untrue thing after untrue thing about how I wasn't up to the task. That I wasn't good enough. That I couldn't build a successful business. And none of these beliefs were remotely true. In fact, these untrue things were WAY more delusional than the true things I was seeing the evidence of.

We believe 100% of the things we say to ourselves, so it is of paramount importance that we have our eyes open to the things that are actually true. This might mean accepting that actually, you are successful already. And yes, you are building an amazing business. And also, yes, you have become the architect of your dream life, and you get to live it every day. It is overwhelming at times to realize just how wrong we have been for so much of our lives because we believed the scarcity-ridden limiting beliefs that our Inner Critic served up for so many years. But it's a good problem to have, and actually the best kind of overwhelm we can feel.

So now that we've demystified the lifetime of gunk, let's talk about External Validation Traps.

Be on the Lookout for External Validation Traps

A huge reason why the journey to your 'more' feels hard is because we still find ourselves falling into External Validation Traps. You might remember that back in Chapter 2 we talked about how easy it is to crave external validation when actually what we most need is to learn how to give ourselves the gift of internal validation. It's how we channel Radical Self Acceptance, instead of always focusing on Radical Self Improvement and the growth we want to see in ourselves or the ways we aren't yet who or where we want to be. And it's not hard to understand why we crave external validation. It feels really good to know we have a ton of money in the bank, or we have a full roster of amazing clients, or we just bought a new car. It feels great when people around us are saying nice things about us and telling us how impressive they find us.

These external things aren't bad, but they're the fruit, not the whole tree. And in the same way that you'll get a stomach ache if all you eat is fruit, if you are dependent on external validation it will control you and not feel good, because you are giving your power away to it. If you are still more focused on the external things than building *internal* validation, it is like falling into a trap over and over again.

Why? The danger with building your whole identity around external things is that they aren't necessarily going to be present 100% of the time. If your entire self-belief is rooted in having a profitable business, how will you handle a deficit month? If you have a deficit month does that mean you are a failure and terrible at business? Or is it just a blip in an otherwise pretty solid business? How about the points in the year that you notice your savings are shrinking instead of growing? We've all been there, right?

But—when you know you are enough, and you don't need to build a business to prove yourself to the people looking on, or to feel good about yourself—this internal validation you give yourself means that you have what it takes to power through the bad days. Radical Self Acceptance means your worth is fixed and is not on the table for discussion. And the best thing about it is that when you DO feel it all coming together—your business is making money, you're gaining that recognition from your industry peers and your clients, and you're getting opportunities that you-from-five-years-ago could hardly dream of—it means you can enjoy it all the more because you didn't 'need' it in order to get out of bed in the morning.

More than this, when you aren't chasing external validation or the approval of other people, you are more likely to get it. It's paradoxical, but we all kind of know that it's true. The world just works this way, and this is what happens when you prioritize internal validation over external validation. When you give yourself the gift of internal validation the externals often show up too. And then it's a double win because you get the whole cake and the icing too.

So how can you tell whether you are falling into an External Validation Trap?

The test is always—how are you feeling? This is a really good check-in to have with ourselves. Because when we are falling into external validation, it feels HEAVY. I often notice this when I start to feel under pressure, because when you do what we do it is really common for clients, and even peers, to project all kinds of needs onto you. It's a tell when you start feeling dark and twisty about building your business, and like you're doing it *'because I have to'*. Or because *'people expect me to'* or *'people need me to'*.

I once had a client say to me that she wasn't going to renew her coaching contract with me because she wanted to work with a more impressive coach. We've kept in touch, and we can laugh about it now, and actually, we did end up working together again several years later. But that wasn't the only time I have felt that from a client.

I still fall into comparing myself to others sometimes, and I see this happening for my clients too. It comes with the territory of being a human being. But when you start to feel pressure to be different to how you actually are, or you can feel self-criticism creeping in, or that pressure of feeling like nothing you're doing is enough, that's the vital time to draw a boundary.

I have often felt like in order to be successful I need to be thinner, more attractive, or have whiter teeth. I have sometimes wondered if my house is big enough, if my holiday destination is extravagant enough, or if a client project is high-status enough—and these kinds of anxious thoughts are a huge red flag that we need to take note of.

Stop trying to please or impress other people. Let them be disappointed if they are asking for something different to who you are and what you do. Let them find you not enough, if that's what it takes. Lean into what feels aligned for YOU. This is *your* journey to 'more'. You cannot let other people's projections, needs and expectations cloud your vision.

Ask yourself—*am I doing this because I feel not enough right now?* THAT is the thing to address, because remember, our feeling that we are too much also flips to the fear that we are not enough. You need to give yourself the gift of internal validation first rather than seeking validation from external things. It all comes back to connecting with your Higher Self and uncovering your authentic self—that is the yardstick we need to be using, not pressure from other people, or even pressure from ourselves.

The Hamster Wheel vs the Rocket

When we really tap into how to stop playing these self-limiting mind games with ourselves, everything shifts powerfully. Ultimately, it clears the runway for the growth we want to see—both your personal growth, and the business growth in your consulting business.

I often speak to clients about this in terms of the hamster wheel and the rocket. When all we do is second-guess ourselves, or worry about all the catastrophic things that might happen but aren't happening (remember, trauma is reacting to things that are not still happening), or ask ourselves *'but can I even do this?'* on a loop, it's like our energy goes around in a giant circle. All the time. It's the hamster wheel that gets us nowhere. And it is so destructive because it means that we lose out on all this amazing momentum and progress that we would otherwise be making.

On the other hand, when you can self-validate with Radical Self Acceptance and you don't need to play that game with yourself, this frees you up to put ALL of your energy into forward momentum. Instead of the hamster wheel that goes nowhere, it's like the rocket that drives you forward as you feel the benefit of the personal growth work you're doing and start to receive the fruits of your labors in the business—money, recognition, and the greatest gift of all—peak fulfillment. We need to remind ourselves at least daily to step out of the hamster wheel and jump on the rocket. Otherwise we are frittering away our time and energy on empty thought patterns that take us nowhere.

So, by now, you can hopefully see a little of why it can feel so hard to be on the journey to your 'more', and why business and life can feel so hard—even when you can also see that in reality/from the perspective of those outside the jar, you are knocking it out of the park.

The good news is that *you are at choice* when it comes to whether these things feel hard or easy.

And now we've done the work of seeing why it can be hard, in Chapter 10 we are going to unpack how you can choose to let it be easy.

See you there!

CHAPTER SUMMARY

- Misreading the Road in Front of Us
- A Lifetime of Gunk
- Be on the Lookout for External Validation Traps
- The Hamster Wheel vs the Rocket

10 How to Choose Easy

I said back in Chapter 6 that one of the biggest shifts we need to make when we want to embrace our too-much-ness and go on the journey of looking for 'more', is switching scarcity for abundance.

If you are looking for a one-sentence rule of thumb that will teach you how to grow your business, this is it:

Switch scarcity for abundance.

And this exchange happens on the micro level when we learn to spot the ways that we are unconsciously choosing scarcity as we go through our day. But what does this mean, and what does it look like?

Maybe you feel a bit guilty for buying lunch instead of making it at home, or shopping at the fancy store instead of buying a cheaper brand. There's nobody paying attention, but your Inner Critic has all kinds of things to say about the choices you're making and the internal rules you're breaking.

Maybe there are things in your house or your car that are broken and need fixing, but you just put up with it rather than doing something about it. This one can be a total lose-lose because your Inner Critic simultaneously criticizes you for wanting to spend money to fix the thing that's broken, while also criticizing you for letting it get broken in the first place or not taking better care of your surroundings.

Or maybe you are starting to sense the scarcity that comes up when you do something nice for yourself. Like I shared back in Chapter 6, my Inner Critic was ready to go to town because I had crazy hair after my Friday massage, and it's absolutely triggering to your Inner Critic when you invest in self-care of any kind. Like, who do we think we are anyway?

The magical thing that starts to happen when we catch ourselves in scarcity thinking and self-criticism is we learn to do three things. Firstly, we notice that we are having these thoughts. Secondly, we don't receive the thought the way we used to. Knowing that you have an Inner Critic, and your thoughts *aren't* facts, means that now, instead of receiving the thought as the truth, we catch it. We are free to examine it carefully. We can evaluate whether it's come from a place of alignment, or a place of resistance. And then, thirdly and finally, we can choose to replace the scarcity thought with something better—we learn to choose abundance.

And the really magical part is when you get in the habit of doing this all through the day, at home and in your work. It becomes second nature to you to Connect to Abundance, Deal with the Inner Critic and Feel for your Seven Figure Aligned Actions.

When this process becomes instinctive for you—and it *will* become instinctive with practice—growth starts to happen. Personal growth, healing trauma, working through the hard emotions as they come up, and sitting with them until they pass, learning to respond and not just react, becoming your Next Level Self, becoming your Seven Figure Self. It is SO exciting when you can start to see and feel this process happening in real time!

But personal growth is the key to business growth, so guess what else. As you start to master this process, you will also see the impact in your business. When we do this work on the micro level, it also pays off in the macro level. When we can remove the blocks stopping you from taking powerful action, guess what the result is? You take the powerful action. And then you receive the benefits.

Like I've said previously, the road to a Seven Figure business isn't necessarily hard, it can be incredibly simple. It's just when you're pre-wired to NOT take aligned actions, it can feel like being lost in the desert for 40 years. When you can overcome your body's internal resistance to taking strategic action, it is being freed from the hamster wheel that gets you nowhere and instead, jumping on the rocket that powers you forward exponentially. High-level clients. High-level impact. Knowing that it is safe to grow your business. Attracting and leveraging opportunities with an energy that you have never felt safe to trust before.

Switching scarcity for abundance starts with noticing our thoughts but has its ultimate manifestation in stepping into your best life, and achieving your peak fulfillment, your life's purpose. And when you connect to abundance and your Higher Self, it is like a direct line to your intuition telling you where you should be aiming next, lighting each step of the journey as it comes.

Allowing for Positive Outcomes and Positive Emotions

One of the most emotional parts of the journey of being an entrepreneur is when you start to see the progress you're making. When you start to notice that you truly are becoming your Seven Figure Self. That your life circumstances are changing. That your business is generating more money than you know what to do with. Success is often referred to as being empty, or a little disappointing. It's true that money doesn't solve every problem, and by itself, money doesn't necessarily lead to greater fulfilment. But I think we are selling ourselves short if we resist the pursuit of success entirely. Success is like lighting the touch paper, whereas fulfillment is the part we want to get to.

But if you're ticking off the items on your Seven Figure Self list and you don't feel the thrill of excitement that goes along with stepping into deeper fulfillment, there's a chance you either didn't go deep enough when you mapped out your Seven Figure Self, or that you aren't allowing yourself to feel positive emotions and celebrate the things you are doing. As entrepreneurs we have to be ready to do life with our emotions switched back on, even when this is uncomfortable. It is so easy to *not* celebrate even our huge achievements. We often despise the version of us who feels happy and carefree, labelling her as naïve or even stupid. It can feel crazily vulnerable to open ourselves up to happiness and opportunity. We feel way more in control if we remain stoic and hypervigilant, suspicious of anything that sounds like it is too good to be true. After all, *'there's no such thing as a free lunch'*, right? But allowing all emotions—both negative and positive—has a powerful impact for good. And we've often allowed so many of the negative emotions—it's only fair that we let the positive in too. We miss out on so much more by refusing to allow the full spectrum of emotions than we do by opening up to them. Even when you're so happy and overwhelmed at the trajectory of your life and business that you're cry-laughing and snorting a little in the process!

For this reason, scarcity can feel safer than abundance, because scarcity is what we are used to. It may feel simpler and more comfortable to do life and business with our emotions switched off, but we can only stay tapped into abundance if we are also willing to go to emotional places that feel less comfortable, in order to see what blocks are waiting to be cleared. It's one of the reasons that it's so important to take regular time for reflection and journalling in business, and to notice all the ways that you're making incredible progress towards your big Seven Figure goal. We so easily miss it or dismiss the signs of progress—especially when we're still addicted to scarcity thinking and self-criticism.

Stop Settling for Less

So, if we are going to let go of scarcity beliefs and replace them with abundance beliefs, one of the most important changes you need to make is to stop settling for less. It's another *'if you say so'*! Stop begging for scraps. Stop choosing scarcity and instead decide to choose abundance.

In 10 years of working with women entrepreneurs, I have found this to be one of the most fundamental shifts we need to make. We are under so much pressure to not rock the boat in life, or to make ourselves smaller so we don't impinge on anyone else or take up too much space. As women we are programmed throughout our whole lives to be easy and accommodating, whether girls, young women, mothers, before, during and after the menopause—women are encouraged to live selflessly and with the needs of others as our highest good. And settling for less than 100% comes with this territory. *Don't ask for more. Don't expect more. Don't complain. You don't need more money. Your life isn't about your own sense of fulfillment. It's selfish to put yourself first.* And of course, *don't be too much.*

My client, Amina was a total pro at settling for less and as we worked together, it became clear that this wasn't only showing up for her in her personal life—it was just as present in her business. Amina was, and is, a caring and supportive family member, but a lot of her childhood had been spent meeting the emotional needs of her older sister. Her sister often felt misunderstood or isolated and had emotional outbursts that Amina would spend a lot of her time and energy soothing. When she looked back, she realized that she was more attuned to her sister's needs than to her own.

And this was a pattern she was busily replicating in her consulting business. She worked very hard to keep clients happy and often found herself undercharging and overdelivering on projects. She came to see that beneath all of this was a belief that she needed to work this hard for people, because she was somehow to blame for any unhappiness they felt. Amina saw situation after situation where she realized had taken responsibility for other people's emotional wellbeing and was pushing herself hard to make sure they never wanted for anything.

And because she wasn't conscious of her own needs or preferences, she struggled to articulate anything she particularly wanted from her business or in her life. But when she really thought about it, she realized that she didn't like the clothes she was wearing or the food she was eating. It was all about settling. As long as she didn't draw attention to herself or invite criticism, as long as she didn't spend too much money on herself, she felt safe.

It's actually very common among women entrepreneurs that we go out of our way to care for our clients' needs, but even though we might be making vastly more money than we ever have, we have drawers full of clothes with holes in that we find it really hard to justify replacing or upgrading—especially underwear!

Western society is very approving of self-sacrificing women and simultaneously very critical of women who take care of themselves. This creates a certain amount of cognitive dissonance for us as our businesses grow and we make more money. Just by the very nature of increasing our personal wealth, we are going against the grain of what women are traditionally supposed to do. When I was growing up in the 1980s and 90s, if you were in a family with two cars, the dad would drive the big car and the mom would drive the little car. Dads had full time jobs and were leaders, moms had part-time jobs as administrators. It is genuinely thrilling to me to see that these days, moms get the 'big car', and there are more and more women like me who are the breadwinner for their family. My husband is the first contact with our sons' schools if there's an emergency during the day. He probably does more school runs than I do, and more of the household chores! But like I said in Chapter 5, this can leave us in a bit of a bind. How do you embody your wealth and success when you have never seen women do these things? I can tell you, we repeat these old patterns because they are what we know—until we learn something better.

The Compound Effect of Personal Growth and Business Growth Work

The concept of compound interest is something we would do well to take note of. To quote Albert Einstein, "He who understands it, earns it; he who doesn't, pays it."

Now I am a big fan of financial literacy, and if you don't consider yourself financially literate, I would encourage you to get smart about wealth management. You'll thank me when you understand the benefits of compound interest in your finances! But I want to make the case that the principle of compound interest applies equally to personal growth and emotional work.

Personal growth and business growth are intimately connected. The things we cannot hold or be with on a personal level will 100% be mirrored and show up in our businesses. Maybe it's a fear of failure, or fear of making a wrong decision. Maybe you had a bumpy exit from your corporate career or were given feedback in corporate that you're not good at managing people, or you were told that you don't communicate clearly. These bumps and bruises are the things that we need to do the work on to heal and release—everyone has them, it's all part of being human—but you can bet that you will see all the fruit of these struggles in your business if you don't do the personal work required to clear them.

On the other hand, can you imagine the amazing return on investment if you commit to doing the work of healing and clearing your emotional blocks, so not only do you feel the benefits in your personal life but also see your consulting business grow and flourish? Picture the compound interest that can come your way when you commit to this work and you switch paying it for receiving it! Can you see your bank balance overflowing while you receive respect and recognition from your industry peers and the wider world? And meanwhile, you're able to hire people who in turn grow their businesses and enrich *themselves* and their families, not through doing work they hate for a boss who terrorizes them, but by doing meaningful work where they are valued and appreciated. I mean, can you even imagine the scale of this ripple effect??

When you commit to identifying your mindset blocks and working through them day after day after day, whether that's with a coach like me, with a therapist, in your journal, or all of these things, you, my friend, are signing up for a lifetime of receiving emotional compound interest. And it will be SO GOOD! A couple of years ago, I had a visualization during an EMDR session of my body where all these deep tiny wounds were coming up to the surface of my skin, and as they appeared they turned into scabs and then into scars and then vanished completely. It was such a beautiful thing to receive in that moment. It came with a strong feeling of deep peace and calm, which is not my default operating system by any stretch. I have no idea where it came from, but I believe it was a manifestation of the healing work I was doing. And even the vision itself provided some degree of healing!

And this is the thing—when you create that momentum of healing your trauma and your mindset blocks and limiting beliefs, it takes on a life of its own. You will find things coming up to be processed and healed that you have been carrying your entire life. Things you possibly didn't even know you were carrying. And as a quick aside, as I said in Chapter 4, I strongly recommend that you undertake any healing work with a trauma-trained and reputable therapist who can support you safely in this work. Many of my clients have therapists and other practitioners who support them in this journey alongside our coaching work together.

So how can you know what is coming up to be healed? Honestly, this part of the journey is so personal to each of us. And what I tend to find is that you may feel emotions that you are not used to or having memories of certain events on a loop that keeps repeating. Not always distressing memories, but there can be a certain feeling of *why did I think of that now?* Sometimes it might be an event, or a song or a line from a movie or TV show. And don't miss the signal from your Higher Self—because it means something. There is something here for you to release or learn, or a glimmer for you to receive.

I would encourage you to get really observant with yourself. What is coming up? What emotions are attached to it? Is there a link between the situation you are facing now and the way you felt then? How do you feel? What does it feel like you need?

And it is like following a path of stepping stones where the next one only becomes visible at the right moment. One breakthrough leads to the next, which leads to the next, and so on, and so on. It is a beautiful dance with the universe and with yourself. It will open your eyes in ways you cannot even imagine.

When we gain personal insight and self-awareness, we show up differently in the world. When you can hold yourself separate to your trauma or your wounding and start to respond instead of reacting—I promise you, everyone in your world will notice the difference. YOU will notice the difference.

What kinds of things can you expect to change? I've gathered some of the mindset shifts that you might start to notice when you are on the journey to your 'more', and you're starting to generate that 'emotional compound interest'. For each shift there's a Scarcity Self version and an Abundance Self version because as you start to shift out of scarcity and into abundance you will start to think differently in every area of your life and business.

Transforming Scarcity into Abundance

Scarcity Belief	Becomes	Abundance Belief
I have to do everything in my business (and/or in my home) myself		I can ask for and receive help
I need to fight to survive		I have already survived—now I can thrive!
I need to plan every detail		This or something better! I can release the 'how'
I need to prepare for hard outcomes by rehearsing all the worst-case scenarios		I can trust myself to know what to do whatever happens
This is life and death		This is fun and play
I have to analyze all my problems and work out the solutions myself		If I commit to the healing work, the breakthroughs will come
I have to escape my feelings. Feelings are dangerous		Feeling my feelings leads to growth and my ultimate good
I am responsible for the emotions of everyone around me		I belong to myself
Boundaries are selfish		Boundaries are non-negotiable
It has to be hard to make money		Making money is easy!

Scarcity Belief	Becomes	Abundance Belief
I have to keep all my internal rules		There are no rules but I can honor my values
I have to believe all my limiting beliefs		I get to challenge my limiting beliefs
I need to be careful to avoid my triggers		I get to explore the glimmers (the tiny moments of joy we often miss!)
I have to track all the ways I'm failing and push myself to do better		I get to track all the ways I'm making progress and in doing so, attract more of the same!

You can use these to get you started, but I've created a special printable where you can create your own. Head to jessicafearnley.com/bonus to access and download.

How to Choose Easy

Now that you can start to see a little of what it looks like to switch scarcity for abundance in practical terms, I hope that you're starting to catch the vision for what it means to start letting go of hard and switching it for easy. Like we saw in Chapter 9, there are all kinds of reasons why we allow life and business to feel hard. But when you realize that it is a *'you are at choice'* moment, we are empowered to do something about it. We are empowered to stop choosing hard and start choosing easy instead.

As we saw in Chapter 3, the key turning point is writing your own permission slip. Allowing yourself to let go of hard. Deciding that you are ready to say no to hard. Because from now on, you are only willing to choose easy instead.

Want to know the crazy thing about this process? You already know how to do it, even if you don't feel like you do yet. This is why we switch our emotions back on, because your emotions are ready to tell you what is a *yes* and what is a *no*. Your intuition is primed and ready to send you these signals. You have already been receiving them your entire life, but maybe you haven't realized what they are and why you need them until now.

Here's a simple way to test this out. It might sound stark, but stay with me on this. What things do you hate in your life and business at the moment? Maybe it's working with a particular client, or doing a certain type of project. My client Cindy spent years doing low level 'freelance' consulting work for her clients, where she would take on responsibility for the 'doing' and work crazy hours each week to provide each client with a completed project. She came to me because she was starting to resent her business, and felt like her life was getting squeezed into the increasingly small amount of space she had left after she had completed her consulting hours each day, sometimes working until 1am to get everything finished. If there is a freedom lifestyle available to entrepreneurs, Cindy wasn't getting it! We talked about her business and what was at the root of why she didn't enjoy it. *"It's because I've replicated my exact working pattern from my corporate career,"* she said after thinking for several minutes. *"I don't get to make the decisions, I'm just the one left doing the donkey work."*

Part of what was creating cognitive dissonance for Cindy was that her body was sending her intuitive messages all day, every day. *I hate this. I feel ignored. This is boring. I wish I could quit*. It would be easy enough to dismiss these messages as complaining or being negative. You might have noticed, women get very criticized for complaining in Western Society, but there was more going on beneath the surface. Because when we sat with these feelings, it became clear that Cindy wasn't just grumbling. She wasn't happy. But this feeling of discontent was pushing her towards a powerful realization. *"I want more autonomy in my work,"* she said. *"I want to be the sounding board for my clients and let them run their own projects. I want to be their advisor, not their work horse."*

This is why we connect to abundance—Cindy was able to identify that she wanted more, even though she didn't know what 'more' looked like. Then when her Inner Critic showed up and berated her for being negative and complaining, she could clear that noise out of the way and experience her breakthrough. She wasn't being negative or ungrateful, she was simply ready for more. She could see that her current situation was not enough, and that instead of feeling like too much, she was ready to choose something easier. Then she was ready to make some Seven Figure Aligned Actions!

"I guess it's time to let go of these legacy clients who just want a freelancer, and attract in the organizations ready to work at a higher level."

Boom.

This is absolutely one of those steps that technically is simple but doesn't usually feel easy at the time. But it's all about getting that momentum going. Before long, Cindy had had some uncomfortable but necessary conversations with her legacy clients about ending their work together and had reached out to a few contacts in her business network asking for referrals. She signed her first $100K consulting client shortly afterwards and she never took on any project implementation work again. She cut her working week from five long days to four shorter days within three months. She started saying *no* to hard so that she could say *yes* to easy.

Can you feel the difference between letting go of hard to choose easy, vs just telling yourself to suck it up and power through the things that feel difficult? Can you imagine what Cindy would have stayed stuck in, if she had only read yet another book about time management, or resolved to have more coffee during the day?

Everything we do in our businesses is playing out the narrative of our inner beliefs. If we decide it has to be hard, you'd better believe we will find ways to make it feel hard! Here's the ultimate test—the next time you realize that you are stuck in your life or your business in the middle of something you do not love, something that feels hard—don't tell yourself to dig deep and suck it up. Instead, feel into what would make it easy.

And don't forget the question I shared in Chapter 6—*what does abundance look like in this situation?* What does your scarcity self have to say about it? What insights or perspective could your Higher Self provide instead? You can go ahead and use the table I shared already, or you can start your own by downloading the printable we have created—remember, you'll find the link for all the book bonuses at jessicafearnley.com/bonus.

So often, we end up with an internal narrative that says, *If you could just be a different person*, or *If you could just be like X person who seems to find this really easy.* But this misses the point, and it's going back to playing the game of too much. What we need to focus on is—what would easy look like for the person you actually are? What would bring ease and flow to this situation? What if you didn't have to climb the hardest mountain or earn it all with blood, sweat and tears?

For my client Cindy, the breakthrough came when she was able to let go of feeling guilty, or like she should be able to make it all work through her own grit and determination. If that sounds like being in the Room of Discouragement it's because it is! Remember, the goal isn't to throw yourself against a brick wall repeatedly until either it breaks, or you do. If anything isn't working for you in your business, who is going to sort this out, if not you?

It's another one of those moments where your Inner Child cannot see any options beyond just *try harder*, or *run away*. But she doesn't get to drive the car at the moment! What you need is to channel your

Higher Self and follow our blueprint of *Connecting, Dealing and Feeling* for your journey to 'more'.

The breakthrough is *Wait, this doesn't work for me! What do I want instead?*

When you learn to do this, everything changes.

There's another potential hamster wheel situation in front of us, though—because what do you do if you don't really believe you can actually have the thing you truly want?

And that's what Chapter 11 is all about.

See you there!

CHAPTER SUMMARY

- Allowing for Positive Outcomes and Positive Emotions
- Stop Settling for Less
- The Compound Effect of Personal Growth and Business Growth Work
- Transforming Scarcity into Abundance
- How to Choose Easy

11 The Big Excuses Playbook

It is a truth universally acknowledged that when you focus your energy on going big in life and business, it is only a matter of moments before your Inner Critic will show up ready to get loud. We began the exploration of your Inner Critic back in Chapter 7, but now we're ready to take it a stage deeper.

I want you to have the resources you need for when the journey gets messy, and it all starts to feel like a grand delusion to aim at having a seven figure consulting business. When you have the awareness of the games your Inner Critic is trying to play in getting you to quit, you are already on your way to beating it. This chapter is called *The Big Excuses Playbook* because we're going to be taking a humorous look at the big excuses your Inner Critic will probably try to sell you—the 'fake news' stories that you may well find yourself believing when you hit resistance on the journey. But let's lean into that resistance for a moment, because there's something important here we need to understand.

The Room of Discouragement—Revisited

You might remember that in the introduction to Part Two, I talked about mindset whiplash and the way it can cause us to flee home at the first sight of danger, OR—shrink down our vision and move forward, but without that same sense of ease and purpose. We take up residence in the Room of Discouragement and it can feel hard to leave. Remember the wall sign in there? *Abandon Hope All Ye Who Enter Here.* If your Inner Critic can't persuade you to abandon the journey to 'more' completely, he can certainly slow you right down. And the Room of Discouragement is the perfect place to do it.

Now I will be the first to say, it is totally ok to have days where we doubt everything, and even where we feel kind of fragile about our big dreams and plans. Where we can't hold space for the enormous vision we have for the future, and where we feel small and invisible. You know when I said earlier that we were going to have some real talk in this last section? This is it. It is fully my experience that being an entrepreneur can leave you feeling like you're failing most of the time. We miss all the signs of the progress we're making, and we construct narratives to explain our circumstances that are versions of the same tale of tragedy. And when we don't know that we have fallen into resistance and taken a seat in the *Room of Discouragement*, all our internal narratives take a downward turn. *This was a mistake. I was crazy to think I could build a Seven Figure business. I cannot make more money. I cannot have what I want.*

But it's important here that we pick up our cliff hanger from the end of the last chapter with the little phrase that can cause the most devastation for women entrepreneurs, especially when you have trauma in your backstory:

What if I can't have what I want?

This little question is one that I have seen come up time and time again for the women I've worked with over the last 10 years. It's one of the Inner Critic's biggest plays. For those of us who feel like too much, it feels entirely logical that we can't have what we truly want, because we have often been labelled as needy or complicated. Our needs exceed the capacity of those around us. We 'overthink' things. When you are a capable person and you're too much, it is the most reasonable thing in the world to believe that we have to endure a gap between what we would ideally like to receive, and what we can realistically expect instead.

Let's Get Delusional

And if you'll excuse me a little soapbox moment here, I have to let you know that the word 'realistic' is banned for my clients. It's funny, recently in my Seven Figures Club group, we had a discussion about how we were all raised on SMART goals in corporate. I'm going to go out on a limb here and say that SMART goals do not serve entrepreneurs. What we need instead is 'SMADT' goals—not quite as catchy but I do think it's better! SMADT stands for Specific, Measurable, Achievable—all good so far, hey, except… DELUSIONAL, and Time-Bound. If we go on the logic that *everything we tell ourselves is a story*, and *we believe 100% of the things we tell ourselves*, it is my firm belief that if you create a 'realistic' business plan that feels sensible and practical but is not expansive, well, I'm sorry, but I can already tell you. This will not be an exciting year in your business.

Entrepreneurs don't want realistic results. We want crazy, out-of-this-world results. We want to do things that other people haven't yet done. We are pioneers! And so, we need to break up with the word 'realistic' and embrace our biggest, most delusional-sounding hopes and aspirations. It's not that you have to shoot the moon or take over the whole world, or take on crazy amounts of debt. But if you won't allow yourself to go beyond what feels realistic, you are going to end up missing a huge chunk of the lifetime fulfillment that we want you to achieve. Like the word 'how', 'realistic' is another shrinking word, and being realistic is the perfect antidote to all the Connecting to Abundance you have been doing. Your Inner Critic is very clever.

It's pouring a giant bucket of ice cold water all over your dreams and plans. And you find yourself thinking, *What if I can't have what I want? What if it's not realistic*? When this happens, your Inner Critic wins. And we don't want that. And more than that, this doesn't need to be the outcome.

Resistance Happens

The point I want to make here is that we shouldn't be surprised when we get hit with resistance and find ourselves in the Room of Discouragement, even when you feel super aligned to your big vision, and you've been making a ton of progress. It still happens to me sometimes. An unavoidable part of what it means to be a human being is that we are always moving between our different internal 'parts'. It would be great if we could just choose our Higher Self and stick with that for life, but we will always be navigating between the parts, like selecting gears or drive modes in a car. And when we can understand and accept this about ourselves, it means that we don't need to be surprised or dismayed when resistance happens. It's another moment for Radical Self Acceptance in action. We weren't made to be always on. A big part of the work of the journey to 'more' is letting our energy increase as we connect to our Higher Self and then also letting it recede so we can rest and recharge for the next cycle.

One of the most noticeable mindset crises can be when we get physically sick, and suddenly we're doubting everything. I regularly get messages from clients describing how discouraged they suddenly feel despite bursting with energy a few days ago. And then they drop the tell—*"Oh, and by the way, I'm sick today."* When we are sick, we should expect mindset to fall off a cliff. Your body is sending all its resources to fix the physical part of you that isn't well. We can allow this to happen and be kind to ourselves because we know that, when we're feeling better again, the abundance energy will return.

Sometimes it bounces right back again, even 24 hours after we are sure it's gone for good.

Ultimately there is really no need to take the wall sign in the *Room of Discouragement* to heart—you don't need to abandon all hope. When you understand that what you are experiencing is temporary and doesn't mean your plans are out of alignment, you can just brush them off, or carry them lightly, and know that you will get your energy back again. We need to allow that energy to drop and even leave us, and we *can* allow this when are able to trust that it will return just as easily. Your Higher Self will always be ready to send you more glimmers, and that rope ladder of escape!

And now for the playbook your Inner Critic doesn't want you to have.

The Big Excuses Playbook

When you don't know that your Inner Critic is trigger happy and works on faulty information, it is all too easy to believe every protest they make and fall for it all, hook, line, and sinker. I know I did that for years. But now that you know how to use my technique of talking back to your Inner Critic and defusing what they are saying, you have nothing to fear. And when you can laugh at some of these limiting beliefs, instead of taking them seriously and at face value, you will be most of the way towards moving past them. Remember, your Inner Critic doesn't have access to information that you don't have. They don't know what's going on and they can't predict the future. They only think they can. Forewarned is forearmed, so I'm going to lay out some of the 'big excuses' that I hear most commonly in my work with women consultants. It's like we've sneaked a copy of the playbook that your Inner Critic loves to use, so that when you hear these thoughts coming through from your subconscious, you can recognize them for the fake news that they are and send them straight to Spam.

Remember that the number one goal of your Inner Critic is to steal your sense of certainty that you are going in the right direction. It's like when your Inner Critic will invite you to stay stuck in the hamster wheel instead of jumping on the rocket, as we explored in Chapter 9. When all we do is second-guess ourselves, or worry about all the catastrophic things that might happen but aren't happening, or ask ourselves, *But can I even do this?* on a loop, it's like our energy goes around in a giant circle all the time. It's the hamster wheel that gets us nowhere, and in the process, robs us of all our progress and momentum.

But when we gain awareness over the fact that our mind is leaving us stuck inside a hamster wheel, we gain the ability to choose something different—and something better. We can instead put all our energy into forward momentum instead of staying stuck and going nowhere. It's like a rocket that drives you forward as you feel the benefit of the personal growth work you're doing, and then you start to receive the fruits of your labors in the business—money, recognition, and the greatest gift of all—fulfillment.

I am going to teach you how to defy your Inner Critic in practical terms, and effectively train yourself to run towards danger instead of succumbing to mindset whiplash or an extended stay in the Room of Discouragement. We are going to learn to receive these limiting beliefs as neutral, shrug them off and in doing so, increase our mindset elasticity and stretch the boundaries of what we believe we can achieve. With each limiting belief, I'll outline what it is, and say a few words about how you can counter this. My guess is that before very long you will become a pro at spotting these a mile off.

Play #1: I can't have what I want

We've already outlined this one above because it's a biggie and it's understandably a go-to for those of us who feel like we're too much. But this one is actually very easy to head off at the pass. It sometimes comes in another form: *I was wrong to believe in abundance. This is all a mistake.* But, ultimately, why does your Inner Critic get the last word on what you can or cannot have? They don't have access to any information that you don't have. They are often operating on less. Look at the information you have. List the things you wanted. Now check off the things you have already received. When we start to see the proof that actually, yes, you can have what you want and you are not wrong to trust in abundance, it is very difficult to sustain this limiting belief. I've noticed that in a lot of situations that feel like a business crisis, we are very often *one sale* away from survival. Better to put your energy into getting that sale rather than getting stuck in the hamster wheel wondering if you're doing it all wrong.

Play #2: I have to be someone else in order to be successful

This one can really have teeth when you're working hard to grow your business. It is so normal to feel under crazy amounts of pressure as an entrepreneur, especially if you're stretching out of your comfort zone. You're getting more visible online, or in person, and setting your sights on working at a higher level in your industry. This is where we are really served by keeping Radical Self Improvement and Radical Self Acceptance locked in step with one another. Your drive for Radical Self Improvement is good because it's fueling this uplevel, but it might also pull you in a direction that says that you are not enough or you need to be different, or more like that online guru who always has perfect hair and a million friends and everyone hangs on their every word. You need Radical Self Acceptance that says who you are is just the right amount, and reminds you that you

ARE enough, always. It's always best to build an authentic brand that acknowledges your true self, not the version of you that feels pressure to be like everyone else. After all, a fake version of you will not attract your ideal clients—they want the REAL you.

Play #3: It's dangerous to become more authentic/ make more money

It's endlessly fascinating that as much as we say that we want personal growth and business growth we also deeply fear transformation. What if I become a worse version of myself? What if more authenticity reveals how selfish I really am? What if more money brings out the worst side of me?

In reality, these kinds of protests are eminently more controllable than we think they will be. After all, even if you do notice traits or habits creeping in that aren't in alignment with who you want to be, you have the power to notice this and to correct it. We have deep societal myths and legends that money brings out the worst in people, and that pride comes before a fall (which we often interpret as meaning that growth is dangerous, and confidence is something to be suspicious of.) There are all kinds of ancient sayings that put barriers to your progress and growth, because 1,000 years ago this would have meant leaving your village, and in the olden days that was a dangerous thing to do.

And the answer to this is really "*Yes, and....*". If it is out of alignment to you to become greedy, or harsh with people, or overly materialistic, then it will not feel good or like deep fulfillment if you DO develop these traits. You can be accountable to yourself, and you can consciously set up conditions with yourself about what you want your growth to look like. You can build in a commitment to give money to charitable causes, for example, or to offer *pro bono* work for organizations that really need it. You can set up an agreement with yourself about the positive traits you want to develop along your journey, and keep track on your progress.

Instead of fearing, *"What if it makes everything worse?"* why not flip the script and ask yourself, *"What if it makes everything better and better?"*

Play #4: My network is too small

I have felt this one a number of times and I have also often heard it from clients. A similar protest is, *"My email list/social media following isn't working any more—it's no use, it's dead! The only thing I can do is quit!"*

I started my business with zero contacts, and one of my biggest challenges along the way, over the last 10 years, has been visibility and making strategic connections. A lot of my clients come out of a long corporate career and actually get client work very easily because they just phone the contacts they have been developing relationships with for the last 10-30 years. Several, like me in the early days, are making a total career pivot in starting their own business so it can feel more of a grind to get it off the ground. Whichever camp you fall into, IT DOESN'T MATTER. Even if you have a huge Rolodex of contacts and potential clients, you still feel the panic rising when it feels like you've exhausted your network. And this isn't a terminal business problem. It's actually very, very normal in any business cycle, especially if you have been operating for more than a couple of years. Your Inner Critic will tell you that you can't do it, but you can. All you need to do is meet some new people. Attract some new email subscribers or social media followers. Ask for some introductions or referrals. Join a relevant networking group. It's never *game over* when you feel like you don't know enough people to get your next client contract over the line. You just need to add some fresh names to the pot. For several years, my husband and I had a little mantra if I felt short of clients or like I was nearing bankruptcy (which was often!)—*If in doubt, add more leads.* Leads are the lifeblood of your business. It is never true that you have exhausted the market. The world is a big place!

Play #5: Clients will never pay higher prices

This protest is one that comes up often for my clients, and it's almost never about the actual prices or the reality of your market. It's about reaching the upper limit of what you have felt able to believe to this point in your life, and it means there is a glass ceiling that you are ready to break through. When clients come to me with fears about their prices being too high, there is sometimes work we need to do to separate them—the person—from their target audience. We often just assume "My ideal client is me, but 10 years ago," and that our hangups are their hangups, but when you charge $100,000 for a consulting contract, it could be that your ideal client is nothing like you.

It really helps with this one to do a small bit of research—don't fall down any rabbit holes!—but get some basic information to counter your Inner Critic here. What is the size of your industry? How many organizations are there in the USA? Who charges the most for this service and what do they charge? One of my personal favorites is, *How many cities are there in the USA with companies who could be a fit for this?*—because the USA is a MASSIVE marketplace for all kinds of corporate consultants. I'm from the UK and when it comes to corporate consulting, we have London and not much else going on. I'll get in trouble for saying that, but it is true from a financial services/corporate consulting point of view. The USA, on the other hand, has multiple cities where there are huge numbers of companies who will benefit from your services. And you don't need 1,000 clients—you likely need between two and ten. There is enough space in almost every industry I can think of for the services you want to provide—yes, even at top-of-the-market prices. So, when you get hit with the protest that no one would pay $100,000 for your consulting services, it's much more likely that this is a 'you' problem to do with mindset than a genuine issue in your industry.

I also want to add here that it is common for clients of mine to say, *"Yes, but everyone I'm speaking to thinks this is too expensive."* And I have to say, unless you've spoken to EVERY company in your industry, all this means is that you aren't speaking to the right clients yet. Even if it feels like you are.

Play #6: I have to work full time hours or it's not a real business

This is a protest I hear often from women consultants that I speak to. Alongside this one is *I have to be at my desk by 9am*. Or, *I have to work 9-5. I have to work the same hours as my corporate clients.* And sometimes, even, *I can't take a vacation, otherwise my clients will think I'm not committed to our work together.* And for all of these variants the answer is the same. When you leave corporate and set up your own company, you get to set your terms. It's one of the perks you balance against the large responsibilities. What hours you work, and from where, is none of your clients' business. As long as you are 1000% dependable and you show up in your best energy when you are contracted to, they should have no reason to ever question what hours you are working.

The bigger picture here may be habit. If you have spent your career working for a corporate organization, especially one with a long-hours culture or the expectation of presenteeism, it can feel really wrong to work less than a 40-hour week. It can feel really weird to work less than 80 hours a week! But when it comes down to it, this is an important transformation you get to make now that you are the queen of your own destiny in your work. There doesn't need to be any debate over whether you have a real business. If you show up and take it seriously, it's a real business.

Play #7: It's too hard. I can't do it

This is a protest your Inner Critic loves to serve up, because it IS hard to start your own company. It is hard to grow a consulting business. It is hard to keep your head when you are dealing with your limiting beliefs and going outside of your comfort zone for extended seasons. And it is ok to feel at times like you want to quit. Sometimes we just need to plan out an escape route to relieve some pressure and remind ourselves that no, this is an aligned path, and it is the thing we want to do.

The question I would want to ask is *Why*? Why does it feel so hard in this season and what is pushing your buttons to the extent that you feel this way? Is it a lack of money coming in? Or are market conditions having a negative impact? Is it that you've hit a mindset block or a series of blocks that you just can't seem to break free from? Are you tired and ready for a rest? Is burnout looming? The key question is whether you are still on an aligned path. If you still feel aligned to your business but you are just really not enjoying the day-to-day experience of running and growing the business, maybe it's time to look at some of the factors contributing to this and make a better plan. Most things in a business are fixable, so what feels like it is ready for an uplevel? Identify the *What*, not the *How*—it doesn't matter if you can't see a way to fix it yet. There are all kinds of people who can help with this. Which leads to our next protest…

Play #8: I don't know what to do

Oof. This one can feel like a biggie. In Chapter 5 we talked about *I don't know* being the voice of your Dissociated Self, and in Chapter 7 we identified that *I don't know* is often your Inner Child, your inner victim, who just wants to be rescued. And whenever I *don't know* or *I don't know what to do* keeps coming up for you internally, it is worth checking in with yourself and identifying which part of you is saying this, and why. Because, again, this is really just a mindset block. But when it happens it feels like a terminal problem that cannot be fixed, like feeling your network is too small, or your email list is not working any more. It literally isn't terminal. It is crazily fixable. Most of us who are too much are what my high school principal referred to as 'Lifelong Learners'. Perennial geeks, obsessed with learning. We are the people who know how to be resourceful and problem solving lights us up. But it's not a lack of information or resources that leads to *I don't know* as a block in the road. It's actually something deeper…

Play #9: I am unreachable

This protest is often hiding behind *It's too hard* and *I don't know*, and it's a really important one to notice when it comes up. Because when you believe that you are unreachable, you stop trying to get help or fix things. Because really, what is the point? Everything will fail. Nothing could possibly reach you where you are. And there are two things I want to point out about this one when it comes, because, firstly, this is the ultimate statement of martyrdom, isn't it? "*Just leave me here because I am beyond help*". I have had clients who got stuck in this and who stopped wanting to show up in our coaching work. It is very powerful when it kicks in and it feels all pervasive. But the second thing about *I am unreachable* is that it is completely understandable that you would feel this way if you have trauma in your backstory. Trauma isolates us. It leaves wounds inside us that often fester even when we seem fine on the outside. And often we are oblivious to the fact that we have these deep wounds until we get triggered and it all starts pouring out.

A good antidote to the feeling that you are unreachable is a simple phrase—*there is always a way forward.* Trauma doesn't have to have the last word. If you get the right help from a properly qualified and experienced trauma therapist, you really can come back to yourself. Sometimes a lot faster than you might think. And with the belief that you are unreachable, I always want to ask, do you *want* to be unreachable? In some seasons, we just cannot do the work, and that is ok. I have had clients finish coaching with me and then come back after one, two, even six years. So, ask yourself, *does this have to happen now?* But also—*What would make it feel easier?* You have complete autonomy over what you say yes to, in your business. You can design it to be anything you want. So, let's design it with your wellbeing and flourishing at the epicenter.

Play #10: I need someone to tell me what to do

Now this protest is also linked to *I don't know,* except while your Inner Child is sitting in a puddle feeling dejected, you also hold a deeper belief that there is an answer out there, somewhere—you just don't believe you have it in you to perceive it.

This protest is actually a manifestation of both internal and external validation, because it is really a way of saying *"I lack something. I need external input."* Whereas when we can practice internal validation, we find it easier to trust that we are able to provide our own solutions if needed. That doesn't mean we should never ask for help—far from it. It's a great investment in your business to hire outside expertise in all kinds of areas. But we should do this from a place of wanting to safeguard our personal energy and resources, rather than because we believe our Inner Child when she tells us we are helpless.

As I shared in Chapter 8, something I see often in women consultants who feel stuck in their business is that they get caught in a pattern of asking for input from multiple sources. Maybe they're upgrading their website with a professional web designer. They hire a brand consultant, and then they ask me to help them decide if their copy is right. Then they ask five or six business friends to weigh in. This is understandable, in a sense, because running a business is overwhelming and there is a constant need to make all kinds of decisions that we usually don't feel equipped to make. But if you constantly find yourself looking to be told what to do, instead of doing the work and trusting yourself to make the decision, this is usually a sign that your Inner Child and your Inner Critic are in cahoots.

The answer comes in trusting yourself to make a decision, even if it's wrong. You are an adult. You are gifted to the point of being too much! You might need to practice this kind of decision-making, but you CAN get to a place of resonance without needing to crowdsource an opinion.

Play #11: I need the secret sauce!

If you've spent any time at all in the online business world, you'll probably have heard talk of 'the secret sauce'. All kinds of things get said about it, from needing the secret sauce in order to have a successful business, to people who claim to be able to teach you the secret sauce.

My personal stance on this one is *there is no secret sauce.*

There's no magical one thing or one technique that guarantees a successful business, but there is a learning curve in business while we ascertain what marketing and lead generation activities work for your specific business set-up. Your business is unique and you are the person best placed to work out what your winning formula will be.

The problem that comes with believing we need this 'secret sauce' (and believe me, I spent several years really stuck in this one!) is that again, we are assuming that the answers can only come from outside of us. Instead of holding ourselves responsible for our business, and owning our autonomy, our Inner Child is pushing us to give it away to anyone and everyone who claims they can help you grow your business. So, every course or program you buy feels like it will be '*The one that will change everything!*' and we end up projecting all our hopes for our business onto this one external thing, or person, who we desperately need to come through and save us.

When we hold the belief that there actually is no secret sauce, it takes the pressure off the business investments that we choose to make, and it also means that when we *do* work with a coach or supplier, we are able to receive their input for what it is—a tool or resource to help us. We don't need to see them as our knight in shining armor. You don't need to delegate responsibility for the health of your business or your own personal wellbeing to a person or a thing external to you. It is always healthier to hold it yourself.

Play #12: I can't change my life because the money hasn't appeared yet

This protest is an interesting one because it often shows up when clients are just on the cusp of a breakthrough in their business. Maybe they've been putting in the hard yards with business development and network building for several months or even a couple of quarters. And they're making progress, having conversations, getting introductions, getting proposals out… but in the meantime, the business is really creaking from a lack of new revenue.

Sometimes clients will say, "*You know I don't mean this to sound wrong, but I do need this business to make money*" —as if there is something bad about expecting their business to be making them richer! I don't think we should ever apologize for wanting our businesses to make us money. In my opinion, this is more than a non-negotiable—of course your business should be making you money. But the thing that I've observed is, a lot of the time, we can actually experience quite a bit of the transformation we want BEFORE the money shows up. And so it can feel unbalanced, because on one hand we are perhaps starting to live life with more intention, making small home improvements, investing in ourselves, improving our lifestyle, improving our mental health, getting outside more and making space for regular exercise and healthy eating.

But it can feel like the main transformation we really want is in the area of our personal finances. And I want to say AMEN to this! But we need to be careful that we aren't refusing to allow any element of the transformation we want in our life and business big picture until the money shows up. We need to show some caution with how we hold money as a concept. It isn't a magical thing that changes us into our Next Level Self. That transformation comes from you and the personal growth work you put in.

This is why we need to make sure we aren't delegating responsibility for our own personal growth to the arrival of money in our business. It doesn't tend to work that way. I have met plenty of entrepreneurs who have made a ton of money and are still completely enmeshed in scarcity and struggle. The money doesn't bring the transformation. It just provides a means for you to upgrade a lot of the externals in your life. The transformation you want may feel like it revolves entirely around money—and I'll be the first to agree that money opens doors, gives us opportunities to create security for ourselves and a legacy for our families. But in welcoming the transformations you can receive BEFORE the money properly shows up, you aren't deferring the arrival of the money you really want. Because what you really want is fulfillment. It's a both/and situation. We want all the fruit. We want the cake AND the icing.

Play #13: The other shoe is going to drop

Oh, this one can really keep us up at night, can't it? I don't know if it's the result of watching way too much TV, where the premise of many shows sort of requires that any material gain needs to be cancelled out by the end of the episode (Sophia from *The Golden Girls*, I'm looking at you!), but it is so hard for us to believe that life really can get better and better on a continuum. And this is a loophole that your Inner Critic will likely love to exploit if you let them.

When we live in fear of the other shoe dropping, it means that every success in your business is received with caution. I have noticed over and again that as women entrepreneurs, we really need to be given permission to celebrate. Sometimes we need to be made to do it! In the Seven Figures Club some time ago, we had a discussion about whether or not it is ok to celebrate when you get a verbal yes on a proposal. Because doesn't that just mean you'll be disappointed when something happens, and the contract never gets signed? Is that *getting too big for our boots*, or *jumping the gun*? (Have you noticed how many sayings and phrases we have in our society that dissuade success and positive emotions?!) The conclusion we came to (guided by me) is that we should absolutely celebrate at every level of the sales process, regardless of what comes next, because we need the positive energy of celebrating all the wins we achieve so we can tip the balance of setbacks and discouragements.

So, when you get a discovery call booked, yes—you should celebrate! When you get a verbal yes—yes, you should celebrate, again! When you make the actual sale and the money shows up, then you should celebrate even more. Because we don't need to worry about old wives' tales about *counting our chickens before they hatch* or *getting ideas above our station*. If the other shoe does happen to drop, you can trust yourself to have the emotional maturity to handle it, if and when it comes to that. It will not crush you. And you know what? You can't insulate yourself from disappointment even if you spend all your time dress-rehearsing catastrophe. Your brain cannot tell the difference between imagined events and actual events, so let's focus on feeding it good news stories. You will feel the difference in your whole body, I can promise you. And failing all else, you are an entrepreneur. If anyone can make lemonade from business lemons, it's us!

Play #14: I'm so weird!!!

This protest from your Inner Critic can really sting, because if you have had trauma in your backstory, you might well have experienced feeling isolated and different to other people. Trauma does that. It can change the way we see the world, and it can open us up to things we wouldn't understand or feel if we hadn't experienced it.

Aside from that, I think that a lot of entrepreneurs can have varying degrees of neurodivergence or strong personalities that mean we don't quite fit in a lot of conventional workplaces or social spaces.

Suffice to say that if you get your branding (and mindset) right, everything about you that feels weird can actually be your biggest asset and be the things that your clients really love about you. We don't tend to like bland people who have no opinions about things. We like people who are bold and brave, because it gives us permission to also show up as our authentic selves.

Honestly, I am pretty weird in a lot of ways. I have obsessive interests in music, gardening (specifically, plant selection and seed planting—the first time I had a garden I planted—wait for it—29 different fruit and veg crops), and quite a few other things. I like the things I like way too much. I wear clothes in all the ways you're not supposed to—too many patterns and bright colors for interest, socks and Birkenstocks, sweatpants every day! I get insane pleasure from hanging wet laundry outside on the line to dry on a sunny day. I do my business from my tiny home office, and I am so content to rarely leave the house at all. But you get to a point where it is so freeing to just own it. I am weird in all these ways, and it hasn't stopped me from building an amazing business with clients across the world who I have a really deep connection to. Embrace your weird. Fly your freak flag. The right people will love you for it. And in all likelihood, they are probably secretly kind of weird too.

Play #15: I can't do it because I am in too much pain/I will never get past my trauma

This is another one that can really sting, and it is a genuine limiting belief for many of us that we will simply never be able to overcome the mental and emotional baggage we are carrying through life. I spent a lot of years before and after my burnout episode feeling like I would never recover or get well, and if you have also experienced chronic illness, I'm sure you have felt this too. I still feel this way sometimes when I get sick. And firstly, I want to say that this is a completely understandable limiting belief to hold. No one really ever understands the weight of someone else's emotional pain, and it is a really hard thing to have to keep doing the work and getting regulated again and again. But this is a limiting belief. You'll remember from Chapter 4, we need to always remember that a successful seven figure consulting business is not a prize you win by having your life totally sorted out. You can be a hot mess AND have a successful and stable business. But it's also another '*If you say so*' moment. It is ok if you have days where you question if you can do it. Let's just validate the expectation that this will happen sometimes. But do not let your Inner Critic tell you that you cannot have what you want in business because of your trauma backstory. Trauma CAN be healed. But it doesn't have to be fully healed in order for your business to succeed, and actually you may find that the two journeys of business growth and personal growth/healing are intertwined. I know they certainly have been for me. Get the help you need from a trained professional to help heal and process your trauma. It doesn't have to go away completely to be defused. But it doesn't need to block your path either.

Play #16: I don't want it

Now our final protest is one that when it comes up, I almost want to laugh every time because it is SO FAR from being true for the ambitious women that I work with.

Sometimes it is just so tiring holding space for our big vision and leaning into abundance, that we just end up feeling like, *that's it. I've had enough. I don't want a business any more. I just want to get a corporate job again and go back to having a predictable salary and none of this hassle!*

And I get it. In the early part of my business, I probably wanted to quit my business at least three times a year. Feeling like we actually don't want the things we clearly *do* want and are in the process of working very hard to get, is often a way of releasing some of the pressure that can build up on the journey. It is very hard to hold a big vision for your future, and the more meaningful your destination or the milestones along the way, the more it can be difficult to cope as they get closer and closer.

I know for me, weird as it might sound, I felt deeply emotional when I signed my life insurance policy and actually shed a lot of tears. I realized in therapy afterwards that in providing for my kids in the event of my death, I was 'correcting' a generational trauma from my family that I hadn't even realized I was holding. In the 1940s, my dad's father died unexpectedly aged 36 when my dad was just 2 years old and only two weeks before his younger sister was born. The whole trajectory of their future, and my grandmother's future, changed completely in a single day. They lost the new house that was being built for them and ended up living in public housing in a not-so-great part of town that they never moved on from. And when I signed that insurance policy, I was laying down a guarantee that whatever else might happen, this particular variant of our family history would not be repeated for my kids.

It was really hard to hold the weight of this action and my anxiety was high for several months. I actually found myself wondering if it was even worth it to sign the life insurance policy. I nearly tore it up and quit the whole process. When our business achievements mean something to us—and I think we can all agree that in nearly every case, it may be business but the impact of the transformation and the creation of legacy wealth for our families is so personal and meaningful. It is natural to sometimes want to pull away from this and feel that we cannot carry the weight of healing a generational trauma that the adults older than us have not been able to.

The question we always need to come back to when we feel like we don't know if we want it—even though all signs point to us wanting it, and this is plain as day—is *"What would make this easier?"* And taking this one stage further, the question I think we often need to ask, but are embarrassed to, is, *"What would be the laziest way to fix this problem?"* It is my firm belief that as entrepreneurs we need to reclaim the notion of what I call the 'smart lazy entrepreneur'. Cut the corners that speed up the journey and stop trying to appease that panel of judges that sits inside your head and tells you you need to 'do it properly'. We already know you will always give 110% to your clients, but not every t needs to be crossed and not every i needs to be dotted with things like marketing, planning and running your business. And for me with my life insurance policy, I realized I needed to stop the overthinking, and just sign the damn thing. And a great question to ask in these situations is *"What will take the pressure off without compromising on your vision?"*

We'll talk more about this in our next and final chapter, but if you're tempted to retreat and let resistance win, go back to your *Big Why*. Why is your business important to you? Why is it so meaningful to you to make this progress? It's not usually a case of what you want to achieve being the problem, but there is likely something about how you're going about it and the story you're telling yourself on the journey that isn't serving you.

We've spent this chapter working through the 16 most common 'plays' your Inner Critic loves to make to squash your progress and pour cold water on your abundance. Which ones resonate the most for you?

It could be that parts of all of them resonate, but it's common for there to be between 1-3 plays that you have already heard your Inner Critic whispering to you, maybe even for years. This is a great moment to get really curious and start to listen out for some of these 'Big Sigh' thoughts that can run through our minds when we're spending time in the Room of Discouragement. But remember, you never need to stay in that room for long. You can talk back to your Inner Critic. It really is the kind of thing where once you realize it's all a limiting belief, it never has the same power over you again.

Spend some time in your journal thinking through the plays you notice your Inner Critic attempting to use on you. And if you need a bit of help working this out, you should consider hiring me as your business coach. Head to jessicafearnley.com/bonus for details on how to find out more and apply.

Up next is our final chapter, *How to Build a Life That Turns Your Too Much Into Just The Right Amount*. It really is the culmination of everything we've explored together so far, so get excited! There's even more good stuff still to come. See you there!

CHAPTER SUMMARY

- » The Room of Discouragement—Revisited
- » Let's Get Delusional
- » Resistance Happens
- » The Big Excuses Playbook

12 How to Build a Life that Turns Your Too Much into Just the Right Amount

We've spent the last 11 chapters digging into what it means to be too much and how we can better hold it so we realize it's a good thing. We've explored what it means to start the journey to your 'more'. We've looked at HOW we can make that journey, and we've even covered off some of the bumps and thrills in the process. But ultimately, this chapter you're reading now is the pinnacle of our journey together.

It's so valuable to understand what it truly means to be too much, and how we can discover what our peak fulfillment looks like and how to move towards it. But the big goal has always been to take this amazing self-knowledge and self-awareness and use it to create the business and the life you've always wanted. A life that doesn't hurt. A life where you don't feel like a misfit or like you don't belong. A life where you don't have to apologize for your too-much-ness, and where you are free to run as far and as fast as you want—or not—and achieve everything that is in your heart.

It's an approach to life that means acknowledging who you truly are as a person, what you feel called to do in the short time we all have on this planet, and where you can make the impact in the world you have always known you were meant to make—without fear.

So, in our final chapter together, I want to pull it all together under the banner of our ultimate goal—to build you a life and a business that turns your 'too much' into 'just the right amount.' Because if you take one thing away from this book, I would love you to do the rest of your life knowing that feeling like too much doesn't have to be the end of your story.

You know like, *Once upon a time there was a woman who was too much, and it blighted her for the rest of her days. The End.* LOL. It sounds ridiculous when I put it in a sentence like this doesn't it? But I am willing to bet that if you're reading this book, you have often been tempted to throw your hands up and say to yourself, *"Well, that's it. I'm too much. It's not fixable so I'll always feel like too much and like I don't belong. Better get used to it. I can't have what I want."*

If you've never fully understood that your too-much-ness is actually a really good thing, it can feel like it's just a tree growing in the middle of the path, and you'll always have to go around it. Or like one of those aches that never quite goes away. Last winter, I was busy telling my kids not to slip on our iced-up sidewalk when I slipped and went flying—much to their amusement—and landed with my full weight on my elbow. There is no discernible injury but months later, I still get a twinge every now and then when I put weight on it absent-mindedly. Being too much isn't a dull ache that you have to just endure for the rest of your days, because when you connect to abundance and discover your 'more', when you deal with your Inner Critic, and then take the Seven Figure Aligned Actions required to get there, you will find that in the land of your 'more', you actually aren't too much any more. You are just the right amount. The parts of you that feel like too much are the right amount for the right places.

But what does this mean, to be just the right amount? How can that even be possible when being too much has felt like such a burden to this point in your life? My feeling is that when you are in a context big enough to cope with your ambition, your intellect, your energy, your enthusiasm, these things stop feeling like things that are holding you back and start being the most obvious, logical things. The very traits that feel like a burden when you are living the wrong life end up making perfect sense for the right life and business. It's like a giant sigh from your body, *Oh! Now this all finally makes sense.*

My client, Regina struggled in her corporate career because she was often given feedback that she came across as opinionated and that thing that no woman should ever be—"too confident." Early in her career, she felt held back by her natural confidence and ability to clearly articulate issues the company was facing. However, as she progressed through the ranks in her corporate job, it felt like less of a drawback. And when she finally left her career to start her consulting business, it all suddenly clicked. Regina's confidence and strong opinions made it the easiest thing in the world to create powerful content for her audience. She didn't mince her words and was able to convey her values powerfully to corporate leaders who queued up to work with her. She was also able to get paid above-market rates for her consulting services because she didn't shuffle papers about and write reports with no major outcomes. Regina can walk into any organization and clearly articulate the issues they need to address.

The very same traits that made her too much early in her career, turned out to be just the right amount when she found a way to take up more space as a consultant, rather than try to be a wallflower in corporate. Far from being a liability, her confidence turned out to be her biggest asset as a consultant. And I have to say that I've absolutely experienced the same thing. In my corporate career I always got in trouble for asking difficult questions, or wanting to get to the root of an issue rather than just sweep everything under the rug. But these days as a coach, it is the most useful thing in the world that I am wired that way. I have always felt like I am too sensitive, too emotional, too just-about-everything! But it turns out this is the perfect skillset for the work that I love to do with my clients, where we explore emotional blocks and create ways to make business feel easier and more aligned.

And I'd be willing to bet that you can probably tell a similar story here. It's very common for women entrepreneurs, especially aged 40 and above. We have often spent our 20s and 30s trying to squash down our too-much-ness, only to find that when we step into entrepreneurship, we need to dig it all out again and we find, actually, we don't need to apologize for it or try to hide it. This is one of the best things about being a woman at this age and stage. We get bolder and more confident with every decade.

And as we step into deeper self-actualization in our lives and businesses, we can also be stepping deeper into peak fulfillment which, as we saw back in Chapter 3, means that we progress to the highest levels of our personal fulfillment. We unlock our ability to make a greater impact in the world instead of sinking into low fulfillment and becoming the evil twin version of too much.

There is also something we can observe here about the struggles we have faced in our lives. Often these are linked to our too-muchness but, sometimes, they are just the challenging experiences we are tempted to wish we could airbrush out. I know, for me, my experience of chronic health issues has at times felt like something I wish I could have sidestepped. My burnout story was one I came into my business feeling determined that I would never share with anyone. It was traumatic. It felt humiliating. I wanted to leave it all behind me and make a fresh start where I never had to re-open that chapter of my life.

And yet—I remember the first time I told that story in my business. It was several years into a mastermind group I was running. Afterwards I received individual messages from literally every member of the group. They felt seen and validated because they had also had chronic health problems or had had a bumpy exit from corporate. People cried. And this is important, because the things that you possibly want to most hide about yourself could well be the things that will create a deep and meaningful connection with other people and also with potential clients. For people who have never struggled or gone through those experiences, it *might* be too much to hear you speak about it but, for the people who have been through something similar (and there are more of these than we ever realise), your too much is just the right amount. Yes—even your corporate consulting clients! They have been craving hearing you share your 'more' and they might never have known it.

How to Build a Life and a Business that Feel Like Just the Right Amount

So, how can you start to make the transition to a life and business where you feel like just the right amount? The answer to this is startlingly simple—you just start doing it. We can actually use our *Connecting, Dealing and Feeling* blueprint here to help set the right pattern. In fact, we're going to turn it into a daily practice.

First—Connect to Abundance and call on your Higher Self who knows what 'more' looks like for you. You can literally make this part of your daily morning routine—stop beginning your day with news, emails and social media and instead use guided meditations or mantras to help you connect to your Higher Self from the moment your eyes are open.

Second—deal with the Inner Critic. And what this really means in this context is that you observe all the times when your Inner Critic tells you that you're too much and you have to accept less. You have maybe listened to this voice your entire life—but as I say to clients often, it stops when you decide to make it stop.

And finally—feel for Seven Figure Aligned Actions. If you're not taking your cues from your Inner Critic any more, or playing the game of being too much and needing to settle for less, what will you do instead? Because what this all means is that it is time to create the life and business that you want—that you have wanted all along.

It's like when you have lived in rented, furnished accommodation for years, and then suddenly you buy a house or an apartment that is a total blank canvas. No gross sofa in the corner with a questionable smell emanating from it. No weird brown carpet that has seen better days. You get to decide—what colors, what layouts, what furniture, what style. You are the creator and designer of your space. You are the creator and designer of your life. You are the creator and designer of your business. There's no *shoulds* or *have-tos*.

We literally end the cycle of feeling like we are too much and powerless to do anything about it when we step up and take ownership of our lives. Instead of showing up as powerLESS, we write our own permission slip to become powerFUL. And in doing this, we can break cycles of generational trauma and generational poverty, because we are putting an end to settling for less and we are connecting to our Higher Self who can take us to places we have never been before.

This is why the Next Level Self work I do with my clients is so powerful. Because in feeling for and articulating the things that we want to be stepping into, we are creating transformation. And when we can commit to this for the long term, I can guarantee your life will never feel the same again. Being too much and feeling bad about it is almost always predicated on a belief that we cannot have more. It's those scarcity beliefs again!

And nothing sends a more powerful message to ourselves than simply believing that we *can* have more. That 'more' is a place that exists for us, and we can get there. There is always more. The world is so much bigger than we ever realize. Remember the question I shared in the last chapter I always ask clients when they're struggling to feel like there are ideal clients out there for us: *"I'm sorry, how many cities are there in the USA? And how many companies? You mean you've spoken to ALL of them??"* The world is so much bigger than we ever realize. There is room for all of us. There are clients for all of us. Your Inner Critic doesn't get to have the last word.

Feeling for the Situations Where This Is Not Enough

In practical terms then, how do we kick off this progression of Connecting to Abundance, Dealing with the Inner Critic and Feeling for Seven Figure Aligned Actions into motion?

The thing I would love you to get super alert to in your day-to-day life and business are all the situations where you get a strong 'THIS IS NOT ENOUGH' vibe. This might feel tricky at first because you will have spent your whole life feeling bad for finding things not enough. This isn't a statement we generally allow ourselves, or others, to make. But remember our mantra from Chapter 1:

> ***When I feel like too much. It means THIS is not enough. Which means I need to look for more.***

The answer has been hiding there in plain sight the whole time. Whenever you feel like too much, this is the trigger—not to blame yourself or feel shame, but—to realize IT MEANS THIS IS NOT ENOUGH FOR ME. And whenever something is clearly not enough, you need to look for more.

When you're confronted with the feeling of being too much, fight the urge to make yourself smaller or apologize for your too-muchness, and instead, hold your ground. This can and will come up in all kinds of situations. I'm going to give you a few examples here, and all we are doing for now is working on recognizing them and putting a label on them.

It might be a client who isn't invested in the full benefit of your work together. They want to avoid having to read a full report of your findings, so they ask for just an executive summary. And they also don't want to pay the full amount for the work. *Sorry not sorry, but…*

THIS is not enough. Which means I need to look for more.

When a close friend ghosts you and you realize that responses to your text messages are getting more and more like 'grey rocks'—as short as possible and conveying none of the details about her life that she would normally share. You'd love to catch up with her fully but she's not available for that and won't give any details about what has changed between you. *Sorry not sorry but…*

THIS is not enough. Which means I need to look for more.

When a supplier doesn't honor the deadlines you have set up, and then disappears off the face of the earth when you try and chase down the work you should have received, despite the fact that you have already paid in full for their services. *Sorry not sorry, but…*

THIS is not enough. Which means I need to look for more.

When a family member cannot be with your emotional openness, and takes you to one side to ask if you can just be a bit more like your much calmer sister, Sally, who never seems to rock the boat or question the level of toxicity in your family culture. *Sorry not sorry, but…*

THIS is not enough. Which means I need to look for more.

When your regular cleaner stops doing a thorough job (look how boujie we just got!—but I'm saying this because this is a scenario that comes up OFTEN in my conversations with women entrepreneurs), and instead shows up when they feel like it and taking liberties with your home environment. *Sorry not sorry, but…*

THIS is not enough. Which means I need to look for more.

When you get asked to do a talk at a well-known industry conference, but your slot isn't properly promoted, and they also let you know that there is no speaker fee as they paid it all to the headlining (male) keynote speaker. *Sorry not sorry, but…*

THIS is not enough. Which means I need to look for more.

When a dear client stops doing the work (though they still want the transformational result) and just brings you excuses for not taking the actions they need. *Sorry not sorry, but…*

THIS is not enough. Which means I need to look for more.

It might sound stark, shocking even, to start putting the proper label of 'not enough' on some of these situations. And I've set out these examples to illustrate how common this feeling that something is not enough is likely to be in all of our lives. If you have spent most of your life to this point allowing yourself to be stuck in situations that aren't enough, it might feel overwhelming at first. But remember—all we are doing at this point is putting the right label on the situation. None of these examples require you to put up harsh boundaries, cut people out of your life, fire all your clients or anything unnecessarily drastic. Looking for more might mean having a conversation where you gently push back and ask for more. For example, *"Actually, I don't give speeches for free. Are you sure there's no speaker fee? Maybe you can cover my travel expenses and make a nominal fee to cover my time."*

I love it when my clients push on some of these doors that feel like they're closed and are able to negotiate some pretty sweet deals as a result. It might be that it's time to draw a firm boundary or even walk away from a relationship or client agreement that is ending, but this is where your Seven Figure Aligned Actions can really make a powerful impact. Feel for what feels right to you in this moment. Ask yourself—*"If this is not enough, what does just the right amount look like?"* And then you restart the process of Connecting to Abundance,

Dealing with the Inner Critic and Feeling for your Seven Figure Aligned Actions.

You don't need hard and fast rules, and you should be wary of the gurus who are all too ready to tell you what to do every day of the week. You don't need a new set of *someone else's* rules to follow. You actually need to trust yourself, to be able to listen to your intuition and develop a practice of doing what you feel to be right and in line with your values. It's like the child who learns to ride a bike without training wheels—it might feel wobbly at first, but it will buy you so much freedom in the long term.

Letting Go of Hard, Letting It Be Easy

Ultimately, creating a life and business that feel like the right amount comes down to one of our big themes for Part Three and the focus of Chapter 10—Letting it be easy. This is why we feel for aligned actions instead of writing huge to-do lists. There is always a shorter path to the thing you want. And in all of the scenarios I've listed, there is the option to just put up with the discomfort and try to make do in a situation that does not feel good vs the option to own the fact that if you're being honest, you are looking for more. You are looking for something different.

And it's fascinating because so often when I speak to women consultants who feel really stuck in 'not enough', they are convinced that it is just too hard for them to find anything different. The logic seems to go—*I want more, but I can't have what I want, and I can't immediately think of a solution, therefore there is no solution, therefore I just have to accept that I cannot have more.* Maybe that sounds reasonable to you in this moment, but want to know something really interesting? When we can shift this fixed thinking to our progression of Connecting to Abundance, Dealing with the Inner Critic and Feeling for Seven Figure Aligned Actions, IT IS AMAZING how quickly brand new solutions can be found. Instead of deciding it has to be hard, we can let it be easy.

One of my clients, Heidi, came to our session one day really flustered about a situation with her team missing important deadlines. She was frustrated with her team for dropping balls, but also with herself—she worried she was being demanding or high-maintenance and, in that moment, she felt like she was too much for them. She had been stuck in a limiting belief for some time that if she grew her team, it would have a really negative impact on the business, and when we explored this feeling together, she remembered a situation in her corporate days when she was told that she was bad at managing her mid-size team of 12 and didn't have the right personality type to be a line manager.

When we examined this further, it didn't seem like the feedback really fit the situation. *"That manager really didn't like me,"* she said. And ironically, the feedback was probably more true of the manager than Heidi! But she had felt very hurt by it, and assumed that because it hurt, it must be true. In her current business team, Heidi could see that two people were struggling with capacity in the area of marketing. And when we talked about how she might be able to increase capacity, she was totally against hiring another person even though she had the funds available. "Is it because you fear being responsible for a larger team?" I asked. *"Yes!"* she said immediately. *"If I hire another person, it risks everything because I know I can't manage more than just a small team. And also, I have no idea where I would find another team member with this specific skillset. It's basically impossible."*

We looked at each other.

"That's not true, is it," she said, clapping her hand over her mouth. We both started laughing. By our next session, only two weeks later, Heidi had got an introduction via her existing network and the team

member was in place and on track with the project. It wouldn't have made sense to look at the situation where the existing solution of not enough team members was clearly not enough, and just decide to be fine with it and expect less. Once Heidi was ready to let go of her belief that it had to be hard, and that she couldn't find any solutions, it freed her up to find a direct path to the thing she needed to remove the friction in her team. I have had clients who hired a perfect fit new hire, sometimes on exactly the same day that we have worked through their limiting belief that they'll never find a solution.

And this is actually an approach we can apply to any number of situations in life and business. We want to let it be easy—and specifically, we want to let it be 'friction-free'. And when we can deal with the inner resistance we have around allowing things to be easy instead of insisting they have to be hard, we realize that it doesn't have to be an 'all or nothing' situation, because there are always plentiful options available. It involves looking at the scenario in front of you at any given moment, and if it creates friction for you, or makes you feel like you are too much, ask yourself, *why am I tempted to say yes to this, or do nothing about it, when I know it is not enough?*

And then ask—*What does it look like to look for more in this situation? What does frictionless look like here?*

For those of us who are too much, we have often gone through life feeling the pressure to ask for less, lower our expectations, settle for low or no fulfillment. The things we want and are looking for create huge amounts of friction, because we are people who have a great deal of insight about what would improve things. It's why so many of us end up as consultants! It is the high bar that Radical Self Improvement creates, with its energy of optimization and perfecting our daily processes at home but also in our businesses. We often feel like—and receive feedback that—we want *"the moon on a stick."* And we kind of do—because we have an inherent love of excellence and allowing things to be as optimized as they possibly can be.

But at the same time, remember we always pair the high bar of Radical Self Improvement with its magical cousin, Radical Self Acceptance, which means we can carry everything lightly because we know we are already enough. We aren't going to throw a tantrum or give wait staff the hairdryer treatment because we got served a drink that wasn't made to our exact specifications—remember, when this happens, it is the Evil Twin version of too much and has its roots in low fulfillment. It isn't what happy and fulfilled people do, or how they hold themselves. It's not about the drink in this situation—it's about being in low fulfilment. And only you can do something about that.

We are not seeking to better ourselves from a place of being wrong or not enough. We can hold ourselves with dignity and loving acceptance, but at the same time look through the lens of making it friction-free, ready to take action in order to create the best life and business possible.

So, the next time you come across friction in your business, it is worth asking yourself—*what would make this friction-free? How can I let this be easy?* Remember, your abundance energy is the life-blood of your business—it's worth protecting and nurturing above all other things.

And there are any number of practical things you can do to achieve this. For example, setting up as many invoices as possible to be auto-pay, both client invoices and supplier invoices. You may have an instant internal protest to this if you are at the mercy of your corporate clients' accounts payable process, and the dreaded Net 90. You might not be able to put all of your client invoices on autopay, but I bet you can hire someone to do the chasing for you. It can be as simple as getting Siri to set phone alarms or send text message for you using voice recognition, so you don't have to tap out the characters, to hiring someone to take care of the different parts of your business. If you're reading this and you still manage your own schedule and your own emails, and/or do your own bookkeeping… I would really encourage you to explore outsourcing these things. It doesn't have to cost a fortune and you will feel the difference in energy when you're not trying to be the stereotypical entrepreneur wearing all the hats. Give thought to how you start your day—and embed *Connecting, Dealing and Feeling* as a daily practice. You may even find it helpful to schedule calls with your coach first thing in the morning (this has been an unexpected plus side of my British timezone for my US and Canadian clients who are 5-8 hours behind me!)—because your mindset will shape everything you do each day. It pays dividends to start the day by nurturing this.

But it also extends to the things we have going on at home. I've had grocery deliveries for the last 15 years, because I just don't have the time or energy to go to the store each week. If meal prep is an issue, think about hiring a home help who can take the burden off your shoulders. I love having a personal home organizer who visits to help declutter my house, and it's been an inexpensive way to optimize my home environment and keep busy areas like the kitchen from descending into chaos! It's also really valuable to think of yourself kind of like an all-star sports player in your business. You are the biggest asset the business has, but are you investing in yourself in ways that make it easy to show up as the best version of yourself? Think about the impact that it has when you are not at your best. Think about the lost revenue from ventures and promotions you were too tired to deliver, or even the things you didn't do because you were too burned out to think of big ideas, or invest in the help you need to keep your mindset at optimum levels.

Because those of us who are too much are often not able to execute everything we think of (I mean, we are only human after all), it makes perfect sense to outsource or bring in expertise so we can be sure that everything is covered. Whether it's coaches, therapists, a nutritionist, or a personal trainer, an acupuncturist, or doctors. It takes a village for you to show up in your best energy and your best health. And, for me, I see things like 5* hotels and flight upgrades as an important business investment in order to keep myself able to show up as my best self when I'm traveling for business. It's not about luxury, it's about traveling without getting exhausted from endless queues and uncomfortable seats. Get the TSA PreCheck. Download the MPC app!

It's a revolutionary way of starting to think about how you do life and how you do your business. Instead of opting for scarcity all the time and just doing everything on a shoestring to your personal detriment, remember our question—*what would abundance look like?* What would it look like to prioritize—and optimize—how you feel, rather than just spend as little money as possible? Scarcity tells us that the money we invest in ourselves is money lost, but what if by spending on yourself you are actually paying it forward and creating an amazing return?

Serving Others from the Overflow

When we make it a priority to allow life and business to be easy, a really powerful shift happens. We stop giving out to others first and looking after ourselves last, and instead we can serve others from the overflow of abundance we are experiencing. Life feels different when we are able to perceive and meet our own needs as standard, rather than just when we really feel like we might be about to hit burnout again.

In therapy, this is called reparenting, and it's a really important phase of the healing journey. Reparenting involves no longer living out unhealthy patterns where we do life on the fumes instead of with a full tank of gas. Maybe you had parents who weren't able to meet your physical or emotional needs when you were young. Maybe your parents did a great job but you just never learned how to care for yourself as a young adult. For some reason, when I was a student, I used to really struggle to remember to buy lunch food for myself. 12 o'clock would roll around and I had empty cupboards in my student apartment and a hungry tummy, to boot. I remember going to a friend's house for lunch one day and she had bread rolls in the cupboard and lunch meats in the fridge and salad and mayo and all kinds of delicious things to go with it, and something in my brain was like, *oh wait, I should do this too!*

I speak to a lot of women entrepreneurs who struggle to eat healthily or to remember to eat proper meals through the day. But remember—you are the biggest asset in your business. Looking after yourself needs to be your first priority. This means taking that holistic view and making sure that you have the food, sleep, movement, social contact and FUN that you need to be a healthy and functioning human being. You are more than just your business. Your purpose in life isn't just to make money or work with clients all day every day. And the ironic thing is, you will make more money if you take expert care of yourself. Because we believe in abundance, this means that when you can be abundant towards yourself in meeting your needs in a holistic way, and this creates an overflow of energy, love, joy, peace. So rather than giving to others *in place of* giving to yourself, which nearly every woman in our culture is strongly programmed to do, you become like a fountain that is so full of water it gushes over the sides, and it just keeps flowing and overflowing.

When you can do your business from a place of overflow—giving to others from what you have left after you have looked after yourself—I promise you, you will feel the difference.

And it changes the way that you show up for your clients, so that it isn't about giving as little as possible, or feeling resentful that they are taking advantage of you in any way. When you feel complete because you are meeting your own needs, it means that you are free to work and be of service to your clients because you want to, not because you need your work with them to meet some of your own deep needs. It's a great antidote to the Evil Twin version of too much!

Pulling It All Together

Can you feel what an amazing journey we've been on throughout this book? Peak fulfillment doesn't necessarily appear for us overnight, but now you know about it, you are ready to set the right destination for your journey of a lifetime.

Now you know that feeling like too much is just a signal that you are putting yourself in the wrong places, and you are ready for more.

You know how to Connect to Abundance, Deal with the Inner Critic and Feel for Seven Figure Aligned Actions. And in doing this, you can uncover what greater fulfillment looks like and take the action required to get there without the risk of self sabotage on the journey.

This may feel like small progress to start with, but if you can commit to just 1% progress on this journey each day, or each week, over the course of the next 5, 10, 20 or more years, you can bet that it adds up to a HUGE change of trajectory.

Life feels totally different when we put ourselves in the right places. When your too much becomes exactly the right amount. When you are celebrated and acknowledged BECAUSE OF the very things you used to despise about yourself. When you can be your authentic self, and know that you are free to love and serve at your highest level. When you don't have to hold anything back or make yourself smaller, because you are free to be exactly the amount you choose to be. Because that's the ultimate goal. You may have been too much for where you found yourself originally, but you are not destined to *only* be too much. In the right places, you are exactly the right amount. And it's beautiful.

We're very nearly at the end of this part of our journey together, but we're going to close with some quick thoughts about what to do with all of the insights you've picked up along the way through this book.

See you in our closing chapter just over the page!

CHAPTER SUMMARY

- » How to Build a Life and a Business that Feel Like Just the Right Amount
- » Feel for the Situations Where This Is Not Enough
- » Letting Go of Hard, Letting It Be Easy
- » Serving Others from the Overflow
- » Pulling It All Together

Conclusion

Well, I promised you at the beginning of this book that we were embarking on a wild ride, and I think you'll agree it has been just that!

We've re-imagined too much and realized that too much really just means you are putting yourself in the wrong places.

We've looked at how we can use the 3 steps of Connecting to Abundance, Dealing with the Inner Critic and Feeling for Seven Figure Aligned Actions to go on the journey of finding the life and business where we are exactly the right amount.

We've looked at the pitfalls and the reasons we can be tempted to quit before we get there.

We've even explored some of the transformations we start to see and feel, so you know that even though it can feel like you're getting nowhere, there are actually always amazing signs of progress to look out for.

And I hope you have been really inspired to start this work.

Whenever I work with clients, we always finish up each session together by agreeing their aligned actions and the timeframe for when these will be done, and setting up some accountability so they are clear on the commitment that they're making. And I would love to invite you to do the same as we come to the end of this book.

- *What has really struck you from what you've read?*
- *What intuitive hits or nudges have you been receiving?*

- *What do you want to be different about your life and business, and what do you want to do to start to make this happen?*

The other thing I want to say is that even though we're at the end of this book, you don't have to work this all out on your own. You have access to all kinds of resources that will help.

Your Seven Figure Self

First of all, you have access to your Higher Self, your Seven Figure Self. She is the ultimate fulfillment of your business journey, and she is a wonderful source of wisdom and inspiration because she *knows*—she already did it.

You can connect to abundance any time you choose. It can feel like flipping a switch internally—*No, thank you, Scarcity. I don't need to hear all your limiting beliefs today. I'm tuning into a different station.*

And instead of receiving all the scarcity, you can choose to view everything from the perspective of abundance instead. It's a great way to boost your energy each morning when you sit down at your desk. And it's a great filter to apply whenever you have a tricky business decision to make.

Claim Your Book Bonuses

Second of all, you have access to all the bonuses that come with this book! You can download them for free from jessicafearnley.com/bonus. They are designed to be a handy companion to the work you are embarking on.

Let's connect on LinkedIn

Third, I would love it if you sent me a connection request on LinkedIn. It's the social media platform where I am most active and where I create content about being too much, becoming a Seven Figure Consultant, and all kinds of business strategy and mindset topics through the week for my 70,000+ followers. Let's get social!

Seven Figures Club

Fourth, if you've read this book feeling like it really resonates at a deep level and you would love to be able to spend the next 12 months really immersing yourself in growing your consulting business to seven figures, I would love to invite you to consider joining the Seven Figures Club.

The Seven Figures Club is a high-level group of amazing women consultants where you get the community support and expert guidance from me to help you overcome your blocks and create the consulting business you have always dreamed of. It's not just high-level, it's also high-touch—as a hybrid program with group calls, in-person retreats and 1:1 coaching with me. Places are strictly limited—this isn't a mass membership, it's a small group experience—but if you are in the low to mid six figures revenue-wise, committed to growing your business to seven figures and ready to do the work of learning how to work less and earn more, I would love to hear from you. You can find out more and apply at: jessicafearnley.com/work-with-me/.

Remember, it doesn't have to be a long journey to seven figures if you take the right aligned actions. And I am here to support you as you gather the things you've learned and start taking powerful action.

I want you to take this away with you when you close this book:

> It's not about being perfect. It's alright to be messy and to get it wrong sometimes. It's alright to feel like you want to quit some days. It doesn't need to look like a perfectly curated Instagram feed in order for it to be wildly successful and fulfilling. You likely have an amazing mission in the world. Don't make it smaller. You are way too much in the best possible way to just stay small and hide yourself away! Go and create the perfect sized life and business for all the things you are called to be and do.
>
> May you find the 'more' that makes your too much feel like just the right amount.
>
> May you shine in everything you do.
>
> May you find your life's peak fulfillment and be a source of goodness and love in the world, leaving your indelible mark for the future generations to come.

I believe in you. You've got this.

—Jessica x

jessicafearnley.com

jessicafearnley.com/linkedin

@sevenfigureconsultant

Download your book bonuses here: jessicafearnley.com/bonus

References

1 This landscape is even more complex in terms of the intersectionality of gender, race, sexuality and class, that each tell their own multi-faceted stories of oppression and martyrdom.

2 White women benefited from The Married Women's Property Act in 1848 which allowed married women to keep their wages and own property in their own name. The Homestead Act in 1862 allowed any household head (ie. unmarried white women but not married white women) to claim land in the western territories. Women of color were restricted from full property rights until the 1960s, when the Fair Housing Act of 1968 prohibited discrimination on the basis of race, color, religion and nationality.

3 The 19th Amendment removed restrictions on voting according to sex (18th August 1920).

4 Oberlin College was the first institution to allow female students in 1837, but by 1900 only 30% of colleges in the USA were coeducational. See Mariam K. Chamberlain (Ed), *Women in Academe: Progress and Prospects* (Russell Sage Foundation, 1991), Ch 1.

5 Title XI of the Higher Education Act in 1972 prohibited federally funded educational institutions from discriminating on the basis of sex.

6 The Women's Armed Service Act in 1948 formally allowed women into the military.

7 The Equal Credit Opportunity Act in 1974 put an end to women being required to bring a man to cosign any credit application.

8 The Simple Truth About The Gender Pay Gap, AAUW, https://www.aauw.org/app/uploads/2020/02/AAUW-2018-SimpleTruth-nsa.pdf

9 Justin Wolfers, 'Fewer Women Run Big Companies Than Men Named John', *New York Times,* March 2, 2015, https://www.nytimes.com/2015/03/03/upshot/fewer-women-run-big-companies-than-men-named-john.html and

Matthew Boyle and Jeff Green, 'Work Shift: Women CEOS (Finally) Outnumber Those Named John, *Bloomberg UK*, April 25, 2023, https://www.bloomberg.com/news/newsletters/2023-04-25/women-ceos-at-big-companies-finally-outnumber-those-named-john

10 Alex Christian, 'Is it impossible to end burnout?', BBC.com, March 13, 2023, https://www.bbc.com/worklife/article/20230309-is-it-impossible-to-end-burnout

11 'The Underachievement of Gifted Students: What Do We Know and Where Do We Go?' Sally M Reis and D Betsy Mccoach, *Gifted Child Quarterly,* July 2000, https://www.researchgate.net/publication/249826897_The_Underachievement_of_Gifted_Students_What_Do_We_Know_and_Where_Do_We_Go

12 Lucy Ryan, *Revolting Women* (Practical Inspiration Publishing, 2023)

13 Don Richard Riso and Russ Hudson, *Personality Types: Using the Enneagram for Self-Discovery* (Houghton and Mifflin, 1996), Revised Edition

14 Useful references are Julia Samuel, *Every Family Has A Story* (Penguin Life, 2023), and Bessel Van Der Kolk, *The Body Keeps the Score: Brain, Mind and Body in the Healing of Trauma* (Penguin, 2015). Also Julia Vaughan Smith, *Coaching and Trauma: From Surviving to Thriving: Moving Beyond the Survival Self* (Open University Press, 2019).

15 Elyssa Barbash, 'Different Types of Trauma: Small 't' versus Large 'T', *Psychology Today*, March 13, 2017, https://www.psychologytoday.com/us/blog/trauma-and-hope/201703/different-types-trauma-small-t-versus-large-t

16 Bessel Van Der Kolk, *The Body Keeps the Score: Brain, Mind and Body in the Healing of Trauma* (Penguin, 2015), p157.

17 1 Timothy 6:10, New International Version

18 Mark Wolynn, *It Didn't Start With You* (Penguin Publishing Group, 2017)

19 This was laid out in the Slave Codes, a set of laws to define the terms of slavery in the USA from c.1640 until its abolition by the 13th Amendment in 1865.

20 Rakesh Kochhar, 'The Enduring Grip of the Gender Pay Gap', *Pew Research Center*, March 1, 2023, https://www.pewresearch.org/social-trends/2023/03/01/the-enduring-grip-of-the-gender-pay-gap/

21 'US VC Female Founders Dashboard', *Pitchbook*, December 3rd, 2024, https://pitchbook.com/news/articles/the-vc-female-founders-dashboard

22 Carol Geffner, 'Ten Percent of Fortune 500 Companies are Now Women-Led: The Changing Face of Leadership', *Forbes,* March 17th, 2023, https://www.forbes.com/sites/forbescoachescouncil/2023/03/17/ten-percent-of-fortune-500-companies-are-now-women-led-the-changing-face-of-leadership/

23 Rupert Neate, 'Global pay gap will take 202 years to close, says World Economic Forum', *The Guardian,* 18th December 2018, https://www.theguardian.com/world/2018/dec/18/global-gender-pay-gap-will-take-202-years-to-close-says-world-economic-forum

24 Eilene Zimmerman, 'Only 2% of Women-Owned Businesses Break the $1 Million Mark — Here's How To Be One Of Them', *Forbes,* April 1st, 2015, https://www.forbes.com/sites/eilenezimmerman/2015/04/01/only-2-of-women-owned-businesses-break-the-1-million-mark-heres-how-to-be-one-of-them/

25 Maume, D; Hewitt, B; and Ruppanner, L., 'Gender equality and restless sleep among partnered Europeans', *Journal of Marriage and Family,* 80:4 (2018), p. 1040-50 cited in Mary Ann Sieghart, *The Authority Gap: Why Women Are Still Take Less Seriously Than Men, And What We Can Do About It* (Transworld Digital, 2021)

26 Alison Rose and Kevin Hollinrake, 'The Alison Rose Review of Female Entrepreneurship', Natwestgroup.com, 22nd February 2023, https://www.natwestgroup.com/news-and-insights/latest-stories/enterprise/2023/feb/the-alison-rose-review-of-female-entrepreneurship.html

27 Fabian T Pfeffer and Alexandra Killewald, 'Generations of Advantage. Multigenerational Correlations in Family Wealth', *National Library of Medicine,* June 2019, https://pmc.ncbi.nlm.nih.gov/articles/PMC6296851/

28 For a detailed exploration of Parts and Internal Family Systems, see Richard C Schwartz, *No Bad Parts: Healing Trauma & Restoring Wholeness* (Penguin Random House, 2021). Also Jill Bolte Taylor, *Whole Brain Living: The Anatomy of Choice and the Four Characters That Drive Our Life* (Hay House, 2021).

Printed in Dunstable, United Kingdom

63363439R10150